Roy Dommett' s Morris

Foreword

In print, in presentations, at conferences and online much has already been said about the life of my Father. My father was a rocket scientist and a strong supporter of all things folk, including the Morris. He travelled far and wide to collect and comment on the traditions he found interesting.

My father's works on Morris and Folk, both film and paper, have been collated and exist as exhibits at Cecil Sharp House. For those who are interested the original cine-film is held at the Wessex Film Archive.

This book is not being published to provide any unique insight into my Father's world but more to allow others who understand it more to build on his work. I am not a Morris dancer of any ability and cannot decode much of the pages that will follow. I attempted to place them into an order to produce the book my father was working on. Ultimately this failed as it was incomplete. There are documents which are entitled 'chapters' but do no cross reference to his computer hard disk in any way. Additionally, there are different versions of documents which have evolved as he got older. I include these for information. There are further editions in the archives.

My father wanted his works to be made available for people to read and use and ultimately develop and change. It would be the work of a lifetime to put them in order. What follows is an a selection of my father's thoughts on the basics and origins of Morris. P

Table of Contents

Chapter 1

ME AND MORRIS

Roy Dommett CBE, 10 Attlee Gardens, Church Crookham, Fleet, Hampshire, GU13 0PH,

I first met the morris at Bristol in 1952 and became a regular dancer with Alan Browning from 1954. I was invited to join Abingdon in 1960, where I went by public transport until it became impossible. My interest in the dance in general was inspired by Alex Helm's work, Ian Pilling, Jack Brown and others. I and my older sons stopped dancing regularly on leaving Abingdon about 1971, aged 38, when for a while we had no car.

Friendship with the Reynolds family led to collaboration in calling dances and morris workshops, including at the Bath University Albert Out of Town weekends. With the University side we worked up dancable versions of unfamiliar Cotswold traditions, leading to a Ducklington workshop for the Ring. Through Eric I became involved in Sidmouth Festivals, learning about European traditions, especially the Basques.

I started filming the morris from 1962-71 because it was obvious that no one else was and the traditions appeared in a perilous state. It is hoped that the concern of people like myself did something to revive local interests. As my professional work eased off, I helped most of my local sides, being happy to share dances, play or otherwise help any of them. The involvement with the Morris Federation came from the contacts at Bath and I tried to pass on the dances that were being ignored and started writing journalistic articles for the specialist magazines. Somewhen about 1976 I started filming again, trying to record the best of the new interpretations. Then after another long gap through the 1980's I turned to video, concentrating on neighbouring teams. However, as always, the attitudes of certain individuals soured this archiving activity.

I had been transcribing dances in the 1960's and 70's and because of the archival interest I happily gave sets of various degrees of completeness to the Ring, the Federation, the Vaughan Williams Library, the Australian organisation, and through Tony Barrand the Country Dance Society. He was concerned about exploitation and persuaded me to put a copyright symbol on future work for better control. An archive helps a morris culture at a certain stage of maturity, then it becomes irrelevant, as has the Bacon book and anything of the early material on the NW, Border and Molly. I only pass out material at workshops, of which I do not do many, and they always have the caveats explained. In teaching at the occasional Wantage weekends the objective is to experience things not to learn them. Of course I continue to read the books and research which helps to put the morris into historical context as well as attempting to sort out what every morris dancer ought to know about movement and being in a team.

My attitude to the tradition grew out of a working class background and is conditioned by that decade of involvement with Abingdon and Bampton and the 35 years with the local village mummers. My grandfather was a mummer, my father in a Minstrel Troupe, my father-in-law a concertina player and step dancer, an aunt a garland set dancer. My family grew up expecting naturally to be involved and now the grandchildren are becoming mummers along with their uncles.

Of course I have helped local women's clubs. It is not a gender issue, they have been close friends. However I am concerned at the ignorance of the past and present by many of the more vocal critics. Many traditional gender attitudes are no longer supportable. The big world out here from whom we draw for dancers does not accept them. I find it incredible that people expect women to be concerned to adopt roles, worry about appearance, and seek male approval for actions, to the exclusion of the exploitation of their natural talents. That they can find self-confidence, self-esteem and fulfillment in the morris says something sad about the society we live in.

The true traditions are based in local communities, conditions and attitudes. They are at little risk from outsiders, unless they interfere. Their common feature is time. Too many people expect it all too quickly, when it is the next generation that matters. I find that the traditional sides have little corporate memory of 30 or more years ago, and often need help to recover it. I believe that they are mislead by, hopefully, well meaning folk. The vast majority of those outside respect the traditions, I do not know of anyone who publicly claims to dance Abingdon, Bacup or Camden, even though it makes taboo whole styles and patterns of movement, which they probably got from someone else somewhen in the past. Incidentally most of my records of Bacup come from "Come Dancing" on TV, Albert Hall shows and the displays at Sidmouth.

What I see as the great hope for the future is that the morris in all its forms is thick enough on the ground that no one can know all that is going on, unlike the situation when I started, and therefore it has a good chance of survival in publicly acceptable formats, without anyone being able to control its direction. There is a joy in diversity.

Chapter 2

HOW IT BEGAN - a 2011 view

"History is the version of past events that people have decided to agree upon", Napolean Bonaparte

In 7,500 BC at Stone Carr near Scarborough, early postglacial Mesolithic hunter-gatherers were becoming adapted to a forest environment. The site gave the earliest evidence of artificially felled trees and of a domesticated dog in England. It also had a set of red deer horns that appear to have been worked so that they could be worn. The site was occupied by only five or six families but the need could have been for disguise either in the hunt or for a ritual. The earliest known reference to a linked-hands chain dance is depicted on rocks in the open air in a valley North West of Luxor in Upper Egypt, dated 3,400 BC, showing five girls holding hands. This was before metal was introduced into Egypt and therefore before the first sword was made. Nine skirted women are shown dancing round a naked male in a rock shelter in Catalonia. About 2,000 BC a small carving was made in Sardinia of three naked women dancing a wild dance round a stone. Megalithic circles were built in Britain from 3,500 to 1,500 BC and many have an associated legend of dancing maidens turned to stone. It is sometimes believed that these circles were dancing areas, rather as the sites in the mountain states of the USA were used by American-Indians at a similar level of civilisation. For the first millennium AD or so the recorded itinerant performers were either solo or double acts exploiting physical skills, presumably larger groups could not be afforded. Surviving illustrations sometimes incorporated performers but they were usually peripheral to the main objective of the art. It is impossible to tell if they exaggerated. Religious paintings often included scenes of contemporary rather than historically accurate behaviour, but they show only the linked-hands social chain dances. There is no surviving evidence in Britain of a group activity that could be a precursor to the morris, and no one has published anything that is about what is indigenous in other countries. Local communities were mostly too small to support teams of young people and towns were infrequent.

Classical roots for everything were rediscovered in the European Renaissance before the Reformation. The Romans had fools known as scurri, which gives us the word scurrilous for very insulting or rude! Domestic fools became popular, at least from Norman times, a list exists for the Monarchy and some other prominent personalities who could afford to support one. The fool needed to be quicker witted than their employer. However, a late surviving joke book is no longer funny as humour has moved on.

However, to talk of pre-Christian roots to what we do is pure speculation. It implies a continuity of form, culture and social environment that did not exist. It confuses the group based activity of the morris with the survival of superstitions and folk lore which are based on an individual to individual transmission and not a community activity. There are certain performing characters and their activities which may have forgotten ritual roles but these have nothing to do with the morris as a dance form or as an entertainment. Significance cannot be hung on the simple fact that people have always danced and done things in due season. Where are the comparable dances of the Celts, Danes, Franks or Saxons in other countries which would have had similar origins? In any case what has been called more recently the "old religion" is witchcraft.

The commonest relevant topic in medieval parish accounts is the church ale, which existed to raise funds for the upkeep of the church, held on both the appropriate Saint's Day and the church's Dedication Day. The typical spread of these dates around neighbouring parishes ensured reasonably frequent accessible celebrations, for which it is remembered that the church wardens brewed special ale for sale. The equivalent of the modern fete, the stalls and sideshows would reflect in part the festive parts of local fairs. Often the event had a theme, first there were the King Games, (games here mean sports) with their King and Queen, then the May Games with a Lord and Lady, and ultimately the Robin Hood Games having a Robin and perhaps a Marion. The traditional songs and stories about Robin Hood often involved falling in water and other misfortunes, quite unlike the modern film and TV takes which do not want to give a knockabout image, and allowed for horseplay and much unsubtle humour. The first mentions of morris at such events show that it hardly overlapped with the Robin Hood period.

The most recognisable pan-European dance is the hilt-and-point sword form and a very suggestive correlation has been made with the distribution of early mining sites. However the first surviving mentions are from Nuremberg in 1350 AD, and Dordrecht, Holland in 1392 AD, and subsequently from medieval towns in that part of Europe that was developing both an independence and a new culture. The earliest British references are surprisingly from Edinburgh, in 1590, and Latham, Lancashire, in 1638. At this time however sword dancing probably also meant fencing displays to music by fencing masters and their pupils which were very popular. But these accounts are for where records were kept by organisations, so were the guilds adopting something already existing in the villages or did the villagers come to adopt what was done in the towns? A likely explanation of its spread is that it was carried by mining engineers who were recruited to develop new sites. There is plenty of evidence that most of folk culture anywhere are survivals from older more sophisticated levels. Also that such cultural things can pass either up or down, but when one level of society adopts something from another, the originator quickly drops it. Like with evolution in animals, society does not reinvent something already eliminated, the potential is not there, however that is excluding our present times with its historically still novel over awareness of the past.

For many years it was thought that the first named Morris or Morisca was staged in Lérida in 1149 at the betrothal of Petronilla the young Queen of Aragon to Ramon Berenguer of Barcelona in the form of a Moors versus Christians battle as one of the celebrations. The Moors had been driven from the town only the year before. However it has been impossible to trace the original source and it is not thought to be spurious. Eventually a form has spread through Spain and then also along the south coast of France and into the northern Italian plain where the Moors, commonly called Saracens, had never permanently invaded but only raided. It is possible that John O'Gaunt really did bring back a performance of the Morisco to England in the mid 14th century along with his Spanish princess bride. It did not catch on. The Morisca evolved in various ways, different places emphasised the martial movements, the two lines or subsidiary characters like the young bride. To appreciate this period it is necessary to understand the interlocking history of these countries along the northern Mediterranean. The international relationships and infrastructure due to politics and trade must also be considered for this period. Henry II of England attempted to marry off his five daughters to Kings all over western and central Europe so that he would dominate Europe. A clue to what they did may be in what the Spanish priests taught as dances to the natives from New Mexico, now in the USA, to South America. The surviving northern forms, still near to their original format, can be seen on video in the Smithsonian Museum in Washington DC.

The medieval church had had a Feast of Fools which when it was expelled from the church was welcomed into towns, law-courts and universities. In France the Sociétés Joyeuse were associations of young men which existed from the mid 15th to the mid 16th centuries with some surviving to the mid 17th. Of the Parisian societies, Enfants-Sans-Souci and the Kingdom of the Basoche, first mentioned in 1442, were law clerks associated with the Parliament in Paris who celebrated traditional festivals and acquired considerable reputations as comic actors and organisers of pageants. They were frequently summoned to act farces at Court, to devise Royal entries, Masquerades and Morris dances. As Henry VII spent his early years in exile in France it is likely that he was acquainted with them. But the first known morris competition was held at Middleburg, Holland, during 1525. The existence of the morris on the continent is signalled by the records of items in England bearing morris dancer images which can be assumed to have been imported exotic materials, just as tourists still do.

The countries of the Moors from Morocco to Lybia along the Maghreb was poor in exportable products and was mostly supported economically by piracy from around the Mediterranean to Western England once renegades had taught them how to build ocean going ships. The Pope had forbidden trade and this was only overcome once he had excommunicated Queen Elizabeth and put England under an interdict in the late mid-16th century.

Illustrations reputed to be of morris dancers usually show all the performers to be doing something different. It is understood that this was a contemporary convention of how to show movements that varied during a dance, and it is to be assumed that they actually all did the same thing simultaneously, changing the steps and gestures at the leaders call. A practice that is still with us and with the Basques. The Betley window, dated between 1509 and 1536, and its copy in Kingston on Thames show a set of characters that have been interpreted as a morris, mostly into the form of a Ring dance. Of course, they can also be explained in other terms. The Medieval Players, a touring company of the late 20th century, performed mysteries and plays and made good use of the postures shown to emphasis key moments in their productions.

The English imitation of the Feast of Fools was led by a Lord of Misrule and such a personage appeared regularly at Court from the reign of Henry VII (c.1500) to the death of Edward VI (1553) and the role still existed at Oxford into the early 17th century. The first English mention of morris was at Court in 1494 and for a few decades appeared where the Royalty frequented, such as Kingston on Thames, Richmond and Reading. Princess Catherine of Aragon was betrothed and became the Princess of Wales in 1487, arrived in England and then married Prince Arthur in 1501. About the middle of the century the morris began to be picked up by the town guilds, for example at Abingdon from 1554-92, and towards the end of the 16th century it appears it may have descended to the lower classes. The existing sources seldom mention who were the dancers. It is likely that at first they were professional entertainers, who could provide plays, entries and other seasonal activities. Such were the Earl of Berkeley's players according to the Gloucestershire Notes and Queries who went to Abingdon. Some other later references say that they were yeomen, the next social strata below gentlemen. When the full national coverage of the Early English Drama Records is complete it will then be properly known. It is to be noted that at Brackley the morris dancers were wealthy enough to give communion plate to the local church in the 17th century.

An analysis has been done of all the English references as far as the early 17th century, up to the Civil War and the Commonwealth. There is not the slightest hint of a fertility-ritual origin. The performances were arranged for the holidays and important events. There is no reference to the blacking of faces, although this was common in the masques. Bells were universal. The costumes were expensive, uniform within a team, and valuable enough to be left as major items of property in wills. Parishes would hire costumes if they could not afford them, e.g.. as at Marlow. Fees for dancers were initially very high, £5 to £25, c1500, strongly suggesting the employment of professional performers. Even in Gloucester in 1553 Master Arnold's Servants, a company of players, were paid 5 shillings for providing the May Day morris dancers, but incidentally 20 shillings for Bringing in the May, another newly arrived fashion from the continent. The Welsh Folk Museum at St Fagins notes how this particular custom spread into that country through following contemporary records. It is possible from the morris sources to distinguish two types of early dance, the first and most popular involved a "female" character and is best called a Ring dance that included pantomimic elements and has a recognisable relationship to surviving children's games. At Innsbruk the women shown in a picture of the ring dance was intended to represent the actual Empress. The other form is a processional, in a column two by two.

The morris is recorded scattered over most of England and maps exist of their occurrence's as a function of time. There is no information that allows of distinguishing regional variations at this early time, but such appears unlikely. Which were the characteristics that gave it its name, costume, music, dance form or behaviour is also not known.

By the reign of James I the morris was waning in popular interest and it was called out in the Book of Sports as needing restoration to its previous position, along with the mistakenly thought still useful activity of archery. The morris had been very popular. In the 16th century Phillip Stubbs wrote how morris dancers sometimes entered the church during a service and how the congregation would mount up on the forms and pews after divine service was finished to sing and dance in the church on certain holy days and festivals. In 1571 the Archbishop of York had to prohibit Christmas and May games and morris dances in either churches or churchyards during the time of divine service or even of any sermon. Kemp's Nine Days Wonder, published in 1600, reprinted by Chris Harris the modern solo performer, showed that interest could still be generated. It must be remembered that then as now those whom expressed themselves in print often exaggerated and did not reasonably reflect general opinions. This is a problem for any historian working from such records.

The first decline in the morris and the maypole is shown in the little protest at their loss during the Commonwealth, although there was no prohibition against dancing in general. After all it was the period of of the first of many editions of Playford's dance manuals, based on dances and tunes used in masques and in the stage productions of that era, although it suited later generations to blame the decline on the Puritans. The Restoration of Charles II through the negotiations of General Monck, of the famous march, in 1660, led to an outburst of reviving Merrie England. Spring bonfires, Maypoles and May Games were enthusiastically restored even before his arrival in London on the 29th May, his thirtieth birthday, especially in Oxford and the surrounding districts. A morris was performed before him during his progress to London at Blackheath. The Restoration left such an impression that many seasonal celebrations were transferred to what became Oak Apple Day in perpetuity, not to change again until the Bank Holiday Act of the late 19th century. By the end of the 17th century it appears that the morris had reinvented itself to fit the new social circumstances of local sponsorship and the associated good luck visiting.

There are several very regional dance forms in England which developed later than the Tudor morris now also called morris. They were often calendar customs that were once kept alive by particular groups, but they were all initially associated with the concept of good luck visiting and therefore were part of the local community and dependent on the existence of a suitable social environments, appropriate to the social stratification of the 18th century and the period called The Enlightenment. Such a countryside has existed since the later 17th century with the growth of independent farms and the houses of the minor gentry. The form of the dance varies markedly over the country, each fossilising a social dance style appropriate to its initial peak of popularity.

The Cotswold morris was as Kemp said in the old form with napkins and bells. It might be better called Wychwood as the teams showing the most complexity and uniformity are almost all contained within the old Royal Forest boundaries as defined by Henry II. This forest focused on the Royal Palace at Woodstock, a favourite residence for Kings up to Charles II and often forming part of the dowry of the reigning Queen. The technical detail is that of Society dancing of the early 16th century, simplified as one might expect of a revival half a century later, but showing little subsequent influence from the developments in middle class social dancing at the Assembly Rooms, and therefore having quickly become a dance of the people, who were uninfluenced by the Country dance until in the 19th century. This is Country as in Town and Country in social terms, not implying a folk origin. At one time it was thought that the morris tradition had diffused up the dessected plateau of the main Jurassic Cuesta into northern Oxfordshire and southern Warwickshire and Northamptonshire, losing characteristic elements as it was passed on, but it may be significant that it did not catch on in the surrounding clay vale farming lands with their different social structures. It remained confined to that belt across the country formerly associated with strongly nucleated villages and the medieval open field farming system.

Modern records research, focussed on local newspapers, shows that the 18th century was the heyday of this form and that it existed from Bath and Wootton Bassett to Yardley Gobion, to Stony Stratford and Bletchley and from Withington to Steeple Claydon. The "famous" team from Bath went up to Bartholomews Fair in London and then provided the entertainment at a major cricket match. The territory may have extended further but no one appears to looked closely for it for example in Bedfordshire and even further north in Northamptonshire. Alternatively the explanation may be that the clothing industry (Gloucestershire), the boot and shoe industry (Northamptonshire) and the brick making (Bedfordshire) which were mostly cottage based activities at that time may have provided sufficient regular income not to require an activity that could be fallen back on when frozen out of work in the winter or exploited when laid off during a slack agricultural period of the year.

Until modern times some of what are now thought of as the morris villages were actually considered to be small market towns. Other local troupes were attracted to their neighbouring towns, Banbury, Bicester, Buckingham, Chipping Norton, Cirencester, Daventry, Oxford, Moreton in the Marsh, Shipton on Stour, Stow on the Wold and Witney. Because sides travelled, sometimes for a week long tour, mentions of seeing a side did not indicate that the team observed was very local. Limington once went to a village some distance away and encountered the local side, which meeting degenerated into a fight. Johnson the foreman ran all the way back home and the humiliation led him to live in Birmingham for many years causing one of the many stoppages of the local tradition. Fighting was an integral part of peoples experiences of life in the past, although no longer tolerated thanks to our litigation culture. Roy Judge has shown in his study of theatrical morris that after 1840 the country morris was in decline as it was being spoken of in the towns as in the past tense.

There were also annual gatherings which must have done much to keep the morris alive in the early 19th century. The Dovers Games at Chipping Campden, until the hill was enclosed in 1853, with the competition at Stow to see who should be allowed on the hill each year to sell Dover's Favours, which were yellow, must have helped raise the local dancing standards, as competition always does over the years. A relic of the Games has continued as Skuttlebrook Wake in Campden. The Lamb Ale at Kirtlington also attracted many sides, and there was a competition here as well. Probably the most common event was the Morris or Whitsun Ale, descendent of the old church ale, with invites to other teams who came with their supporters to meet the Lord and Lady of the Ale, who then escorted them to examine the antiquities which had been given fanciful names that had to be guessed, with the possibility of incurring penalties or forfeits including a ride on the wooden horse. Quite early the morris was selling printed rag paper tabards and bows or rosettes in local colours to supporters, the modern tee shirts and buttons are not really new! The loss of the major gatherings and the rise of competing activities was followed by the folding of many traditional troupes as part of the Victorian restructuring of community life.

The morris had been partially supported by the new opportunities that existed in the 19th century. Nearly every village had its own Friendly Society with its annual walk, church service, feast and subsequent entertainments. But other events which were becoming regular such as flower and produce shows had problems with the remembered 18th century behaviour that the morris evoked, of sexual permissiveness, drink and riot. Increased mobility, emigration, the attraction of the growing towns and the lack of leisure time from industrialisation, plus the changing social attitudes of the growing middle classes, all discouraged younger people from keeping it up. As some old dancers complained, it had got like begging. However there were revivals of village teams, some to support national celebrations, others because of an apparent growth in local support, and eventually in the growing antiquarian interest in older behaviours with the invention of the concepts of "tradition" and "folk". On the whole there had to be an element of sponsorship for this to happen. Unfortunately most available 20th century histories have been written from the other side of the fence, aimed at being eulogies of those who promoted the collected material, and not as seen by the dancers involved.

Consequently their human faults are seldom mentioned, although important to understanding their times.

"Until lions have their historians, tales of the hunt shall always glorify the hunter", Nigerian proverb.

In Northamptonshire it overlapped with the Midland or Bedlam morris which appears to have been spread from Northampton to the Welsh Border and from the Vale of Evesham to Shropshire. This was a mid winter activity and tradesmen maintained it with the chief characteristic of the regular clashing of sticks. It may have emphasised complex rhythmic noises rather than a melody line. The combat aspect of the Morisca had developed in Italy into the Matachins and spread in popularity to France, Spain and then England in the later half of the 16th century. The first English references at Court are in 1582-3 to 1590. A description was published by Arbeau in 1589, showing the use of simple fencing movements and clearly a forerunner of dances shown by many continental sides today. There appears to be a confusion over fencing like actions and the quite different morris which appealed to antiquarians looking for explanations. In Northamptonshire in the 18th century the two forms were clearly distinguished, but the use of sticks in the Cotswold dance appears to have diffused southwards.

The so called Border Morris, a title invented since 1970 when there was a January Instructional at Ledbury sponsored by the West Midland Folk Federation, is represented by a dozen collected dances which have little in common, other than that modern sides ignore them. Their characteristic was the use of rather short sticks or possibly trade instruments, and a great variety of costumes, quite unlike the modern rag jacket inventions. Precision not power was a characteristic, no one doubted the strength of the Agricultural Labourer but precision teamwork was a novelty. The current troupes now commonly have bands whose music and dancers blacked up faces appear to owe much to the immense popularity of black faced minstrelsy after 1843 when the first "Ethiopian" troupe from the USA amazed Europe. Between the world wars amateur companies were common and popular and often replaced mummers and other traditional behaviours throughout the country. Such groups have found an unfilled niche, but do make historical claims that will be hard to prove.

In the 18th century all popular antiquities. as they were then called, were viewed as survivals of classical mythology. In the 19th they were all given Scandinavian origins. The folk revival looked for a history that was indigenous and lost in the mists of time. Today we are not surprised if fashions come and go. But fashion is innovative, whereas the traditional process is selective. The origin is not important but the use to which it is put is. The modern morris scene is not a survival of what existed in the 19th century but yet another reinvention of its use to fit it to today. As society continues to change so will the morris, as it always has done.

The topics covered are selected from a wide ranging check list of possible influences on the English Morris. There are no studies of entire communities to show whether the morris dancers past or present were exceptional in any way. The best that can be observed are the modern non-elite teams of local people with ordinary backgrounds.

The recovery of some of the dances and the reinvention of the morris for the 20th century is another story. It became part of the long struggle for equality which went from abolishing slavery, to the gap between rich and poor, and then the rights of women.

ANNEX : A HISTORICAL ACCOUNT OF THE MORRIS

G Rowell wrote in "Notes on Some Old-Fashioned English Customs" in Folk Lore, Vol 4 part 2 1886.

"So long as Morris dancing was kept up with spirit, ie, to about 1830 or 1840, there was a sort of rivalry in parishes as to which should have the best turn-out, so that the six selected were generally the pick of the parish for activity and appearance. Their dress, if well got up, was uniform, ie, no waistcoat, white linen shirt of good quality pleated and got up in the best style. A broad ribbon from each shoulder was crossed on the breast and back and, terminating at the waist, the ends formed a sort of sash. Small bows of narrow ribbon were fixed on the crossing of the wider ribbon, the shoulders, the wrists, and the upper arms; the colours were sometimes various, but generally those of the nobleman or leading family of the parish. Small bells, producing a sort of jingling sound, attached to the coloured bindings, were fastened around the legs below the knee and above the ankles. Black beaver hat of good quality. From the above, considering the times to which I refer, it may be seen that starting a morris, complete on all points, was rather costly.

The dances were in various forms, but in all the six had to move in unison; sometimes with a white handkerchief in one or both hands waved about in various manners; in other dances there was a clapping of hands, either by each bringing the palms together or by each meeting those of his partner; and, in others, each had a staff of abou- two feet in length, and these were flourished and clashed together in various ways. There was no display of "footing" in the dancing, but the great aim seemed to be to keep the time and figure, so that every sound and every movement should be strictly in unison. The music was the simple tabor and pipe, and these probably merely to mark the time: the use of the fiddle in late years seemed quite an inappropriate innovation.

My memory will go fairly back to the first decade of the century [19th] but I have no remembrance of seeing any representation of Maid Marion in connection with the Morris dance, and I see no grounds for mixing up this dance with the Robin Hood characters otherwise than for their being popular amusements of the same times. The clown I have always known in connection with the Morris dance, but it is probable that this was merely an adoption of the domestic fool from necessity. There was nothing in his get-up to connect him to the dance - he was merely grotesque. He had a stick of about three feet in length with a calf's tail fastened on one end and an inflated bladder suspended at the other, and in the use of it he was privileged. He made very free use of this in clearing and keeping a space for the dancers and in his endeavours to raise a laugh one of the most successful being in the dexterous manner in which he could take a man's hat off by a mere whisk of the calf's tail, or bonnet him by bringing his hat down over his eyes by a blow from the bladder. For such tricks as these, as with the domestic fool, rough as they were, he had full immunity in the general privilege of the clown.

The evidence from Churchwarden's accounts and other statements, given in Brand's 'Popular Antiquities' (1873), shows that these and similar pastimes originated or were adopted - at least in some cases - as a means for raising money for parochial and charitable purposes .... At meetings called for such purposes, even the highest in a parish might attend with propriety, and could hardly avoid doing so, and, doubtless, under such circumstances, the choice of lord and lady (or May Queen) would fall on the apparently most deserving, thus becoming an honour to be wished for. 'At present', says Diouce, quoting from Rudder (Brand Vol 1 p 279), 'the Whitsun Ales are conducted in the following manner:- Two persons are chosen, previous to the meeting to be lord and lady of the ale, who dress suitably as they can to the character they assume. A large empty barn, or some such building is provided for the lord's hall and fitted with seats to accommodate the company. Here they assemble to dance and regale in the best manner their circumstances and place will afford, and each young fellow treats his girl with a ribbon or favour. The lord and lady honour the hall with their presence attended by the steward, sword-bearer, purse-bearer, and mace-bearer with their several badges or ensigns of office. (The mace is made of silk finely plaited, with ribands on the top and filled with spices and perfumes for such of the company to smell as desire it). They have likewise a trainbearer or page, and a fool or jester, drest in a party-coloured jacket, whose ribaldry and gesticulations contribute not a little to the entertainment of some of the company. The lord's music, consisting of a pipe and tabor, is employed to conduct the dance'.

Bearing in mind that in those times bear-baiting, morris-dancing, and the like were royal amusements, it may well be imagined that such meetings as those above described were pleasurable in a high degree, and thus Whitsun-Ales were continued long after the causes which had given rise to them had ceased; but, being carried on merely for profit or sport, degenerated into amusements of a more rollicking and boisterous character than those of the earlier times. However, since the earlier part of the present century [19th] when they were not infrequent, they have altogether ceased, so that there are not many who now know the meaning of the name, which must soon pass altogether out of remembrance.

Under these circumstances the following description of the most recent period may be interesting:-

A large barn was fitted up with seats for the company, and called my lord's hall; a portion for the sale of beer, etc, was called my lord's buttery; and another portion, fitted up with branches and flowers for the sale of cakes and confectionary, was called my lady's bower. Owls were hung about in cages and called my lord's parrots;

other song less birds, as the rook, jackdaw, raven, or the like, were called my lady's nightingales; and anyone using a name for these and other objects otherwise than that thus given them became liable to a fine, with a ride on the wooden-horse or my lord's charger. The lord and lady, with their male and female attendants, all gaily dressed and bedecked with ribbons, were free in their offers of flowers or cake, for the acceptance of which the fee was expected. The wooden-horse, the principal source for amusement, was a stout pole, elevated on four legs to a convenient height, with a small platform on which the lady's chair was fixed and the man could set his feet as he sat astride the pole. Every man who paid the fine was privileged to mount the horse and be carried round the boundaries, with the lady seated before him, with kisses unlimited. If a female paid forfeit she took the lady's place, and the lord had to mount and do the kissing part. But if a man would not pay in money he had to mount the horse per force and alone, with a practical lesson in rough-riding which he would not readily forget. It was not however altogether as a fine that the money was paid as men and mere boys would intentionally incur the penalty to boast of their ride on the charger and kissing the lady, and many females for mere frolic would follow suit. There were morris-dancings and other amusements; but enough has been said to show that, whatever we may think of the Whitsun-Ales of olden times, there is not much to regret in their suppression in the later period."

FURTHER READING

The social changes over 500 years to which the morris has had to adjust have been very large, but direct evidence of what this has meant is rare. However there are considerable sources for the social conditions over this period within which the morris has had to operate, except for the last 30-40 years with the enormous growth of activity which is unfortunately poorly documented. Perhaps the most relevant or most interesting is the developments in "popular culture" and how this has driven and been exploited by commercialisation. An insightful text is that originally written for the Open University.

J M Golby   The Civilisation of the Crowd - Popular Culture in England 1750-1900

A Purdue   Sutton Publishing, Stroud, 1999 edition. ISBN 0 7509 2178 1

Although the growth of sports and alternative activities has been researched, the impact on the decline of traditional pastimes is much less developed. The phenomena of the amazing growth of the morris post war has not been examined and there is a considerable risk that the story will be lost as the participants fade away, leaving what are largely myths about how it developed. We need some case histories of clubs and morrisographies of some of the influential personalities.

MY THOUGHTS ON THE MORRIS, ITS EARLY HISTORY AND ORIGINS

by Roy Dommett, Friend of the Morris Federation, from a Sidmouth Lecture

KEY STARTING POINTS

The performing arts are ephemeral, and, like religions, needing to be constantly recreated to exist. This allows them to adjust over time to changing external social and cultural circumstances, as well as to internal choices.

Morris is defined here as the public outdoor performance mostly accompanied by music by a group of costumed and rehearsed dancers for entertainment and consequent voluntary reward. It excludes what are inward looking local customs, like beating the bounds, or town rides. There is no evidence of the survival in Britain of primitive community hunting or fertility dances as might have been performed by men and women respectively. This is hardly surprising considering the history of the country which has been one of constant change.

Today this definition could include groups from dance schools, Can-Can dancers, Egyptian Belly dancers, Bengali dancers with material based on Bollywood films, and other ethnic teams. I do not exclude the weird and wonderful or the avante garde, but these have to stand or fall on their own merits. The morris today implies some roots in distant past performances, although this cannot always have been so! The morris often exploits nostalgia in its appearnace and behaviour to preserve past idioms and attitudes as long as they are still socially acceptable. Hence the difficulties that have arisen when some changes of uncertain future or value have occurred. The most obvious of these has been the reacceptance of women as proper heirs of the tradition.

The morris is unique in Britain in that it goes out to find its audience, which does not have to pay to watch, although the performers can be engaged for fund raising and celebratory events. It is often in its impact more carnival than artistic.

The morris is an event and accounts about it should properly be about its performance, not its history. For some intellectual reason its origins have appeared to be important, perhaps this is the fault of the propaganda thought necessary by the original revivalists, however it has not helped our cause and it contributes to the continuing dubious public image which has existed ever since World War One.

Of course you can believe what you like about the past, unless it affects your behaviour and any decisions that impinge on other people. The historic truth is hard to ascertain, but perhaps we are getting close to posing the right questions! However there is a difference between the imagined Past and the actual History which will have to be discussed later.

The accessibility of public records nowadays provides information about the lives of former dancers and musicians, but it does little for our understanding of the morris as an event or as dances in their traditional context. Even if it could, it is unlikely to provide a guide to what it is or could be today. There is perhaps a need to appreciate the social and cultural changes that have occured, if only to recognise that attitudes and behaviour common in the past may no longer be appropriate or acceptable.

TOWARDS A THEORY OF THE MORRIS

Human behaviour is inordinately complex, but a satisfactory theoretical background for the morris has to answer four key questions, for a serious discussion with critics.

a   Why do humans engage in such activities? We have no real idea whether morris like activities or organised religion came first. Immediately after the last Ice Age the country was empty. Settlers in a new country have always been pragmatic and responded to what appeared to them to be useful quickly or basic, whereas religions needed to develop intellectual concepts and to persuade other people. The potential for a conflict has periodically raised intellectual problems because, although initially neutral, leisure activities have naturally always attracted local religious overtones, leading to suspicions of the continuity of its propriety when there were major cultural changes, such as when the Roman Empire became predominantly Christian, or part of the Catholic world became Protestant.

b   Does it account for its persistence through the various stages of our society's development? Since folk culture was first recognised as such it was assumed to be essentially conservative in the long term, even if there are periods of cutting edge creativity. The oral tradition implied is essentially a 'grandfather rule' as accessibility to the tradition is inherently limited by existing memories. Is modern recording and archiving distorting the process?

c   Can it explain the apparent diversity of activities under the common title? Is there a universal element? Why do they do it? Why is performance often as simple as it can be to achieve the objective? There has been in the past a basic urge to perform which adopts the local idiom, but in such a   manner that each area exhibits similar motivation and conduct.

d   What is it role today? What do its participants and audience gain to make it worth continuing? Group rhythmic activity is uplifting, the cheerful attitudes generate 'feel good' factors, the physiological effects are significant, if not understood properly. But growing up within a morris team environment does not necessarily prepare dancers for the wider world.

These questions involve fundamental issues of continuity, leisure, clubs, and gender which have a wider significance. But morris' history ought to be able to be used to support the conclusions from any such larger debate, which will unfortunately have to be persued elsewhere.

The problem with tradition is that it gradually erodes, so it also depends on a degree of creativity and on performers of exceptional ability who reinvigorate the content. The difficulty with preserving by oral transmission, or in our case by word of foot, is that complexities of technique as distinctive features often become lost because of the technical limitations of those who are trying to transmit it to others. These recipents in turn will not have access to any group from whom to derive any concepts of the degree of tolerance of variation or of excellence that had been acceptable within the original source.

Teachers or transmitters have of necessity to be selective in what is passed on. This involves value judgements which must inadvertently produce a drift in how movements are done.

Morris is yet another form of sport, in its modern existance it is seldom competitive except in the friendliest way. The past arguments used for its 'ritual' origins also apply to older sports in general. As a folk custom it is a community based activity, unlike folk song, story telling or superstitions, which are often transmitted uncritically by one-to-one contact.

2   "The Revival" - THE CONFUSION CAUSED BY RECEIVED HISTORY

Too much of what may have existed as explanation in the early twentieth century has been misleading. For many years it was stated that, and the quotes are from Stephen Corrsin in his book on Sword Dances,

"A few well educated middle and upper class English men and women rescued and preserved priceless jewels of English folk dance and music from degeneration and disappearance; they were able to collect and teach these jewels with unique accuracy; and they did so selflessly, without motives of personal advancement or support for particular political and social ideologies."

This activity was justified by pseudo science. It has been convenient to airbrush out its modern reinvention in real social concerns, including the activities involved with opposition to the Boer War, Votes for Women, the early Fabian Society and the early members of the Parliamentary Labour Party all at the start of the twentieth century.

"Sharp and other revivalists found intellectual support in the theory of primitive 'survivals in Culture' developed by E Tylor, long discarded by scholars, but not by the revival itself."

It has been very difficult to get people to reject the images of Frazer's "Golden Bough", as well as ignoring the unspoken consequential assumptions of subsequent collectors. It focussed attention into the wrong areas when people started looking for evidence. All of which has distorted our understandings of what had actually happened.

"The collectors were deeply involved and active in their own societies. Their attitudes had critical impacts, for example, the morris should be rural and male. The role of women was unrepresented and in the revival marginalised, trivialised or ignored. There was a right wing bias until well after WWII."

Much more can be made of the apparent errors, superficialities and absurdities of past literature which often reflected the common understanding of the academic attitudes of the times, that have now yielded to scientific study in more recent years. It is better to accept that it occurred and then ignore it as irrelevant for today. Between the wars, the morris was organised and preserved in a Middle Class determined context, but without that phase it would not have existed to be rediscovered since World War II.

Of course, when examining it in detail, nothing was really revived or replicated, neither the people, their condition, the costumes, the occasions, the instruments or implements. It was reinvented, eventually as dance troupes in a club or class atmosphere and usually in a year round weekly environment! We also lack evidence now for the fidelity of the transmission of what we think has been preserved, because of the limitations of all movement notations.

3   THE EXTRAPOLATION BACK

The recognised professional approach to history, as advised for those constructing family history, is to work in reverse, starting from the recent and working steadily further back. History is recorded in either oral or documentary formats. Oral history has many recognised and well documented shortcomings, memories are neither perfect nor cover all that is relevant, but it does avoid the problem with interpreting old contemporary written material which should always to be considered in the light of who is writing what to whom to achieve which effect, now subject to what is often called spin. One problem is that some of what are actually the key issues were thought of as so common and understood by everyone that they did not get mentioned at all.

This point raises again the question of the fundamental difference between 'History' and the 'Past'. The former is the facts that can be established and is inherently full of gaps which published narrative accounts have to gloss over. This is why they are called Secondary Sources. The later is that which is imagined or assumed and is what is normally used to guide activities and decisions and is not necessarily a true reflection of what actually happened. A narrative can utilise a wider base of knowledge than could have been available to the individual participants at the time, but it does not know what it does not know, and is therefore subject to revisionists who have perhaps obtained more detail or a more insightful approach. The usual result is that revisionists are able to make situations appear to have been more complex and past interpretations to have been too simplistic.

That things in the past changed is beyond dispute, just think of the personal mental images associated with mentions of the Stone Age, Romans, Saxons, Normans, Tudors, Restoration, Victorians and even the 1930's, or if you are old enough, what you have lived through yourself.

Changes are just as significant when considering much shorter intervals. Relevant to the morris, and roughly speaking,

2000   Documentation of popular culture,

1950   Rediscovery by educated working class,

1900   Social reform, Fabians, Labour Party and Suffragettes, leading to a so called Revival,

1850   Rational Activities and redefining Women's Place, the killing of traditional behaviours,

1800   Napoleonic Wars and social disruptions, leading to economic necessities not good luck visits,

1750   American Rebellion and the Enlightenment, deference and the presumed heyday of traditions,

1700   The Glorious Revolution, really being conquered by the Dutch, with the start of a reinvention of culture after the Civil Wars, the Protectorate and the Restoration. An age when deference was a normal imposed part of life.

It was impossible to ignore the changes in society over the years and the morris as an event has had to adjust to remain acceptable or tolerable. The dance forms surviving were regional and each idiom naturally has a different history, reflected in its character and its performance.

Cotswold - Keith Chandler's publications show the continuity back to 1700, but few very long lifed teams and there was a dependence for existence on external factors such as local patronage, ales, and clubs such as the Friendly Societies from late 18th century.

Molly, Stave - mid to late 19th C, contemporary country dance like.

Salisbury - an occasional morris out with the Giant and Hobnob the hobby horse on national celebration occasions.

Long Sword - the European analogues peaked before England had examples, and they had a greater variety of movements.

Rapper - needed the invention of flexible spring steel to be done, with an economy of numbers.

Border - not very country dance like. Used very short sticks or work implements, aimed at showing precision not strength, unlike today.

4   EARLY MORRIS OPPORTUNITIES

This actually means here the pre 1800 period, before any oral evidence was available to the first collectors. But all the dance forms found later depended on local functions that no longer exist now as common living community activities, and many cannot be traced back before 1800, typically,

Cotswold - Ales and Clubs

Processionals - Rushcarts

Border, Molly, Long Sword - Mid Winter Slack Times

Stave - Friendly Society Annual Walk

Rapper - Pubs and Clubs Tours

Seasonal Plays - Patronage, outdoor and indoor performance styles

All were dying out in 19th Century, many of those left ended with the slaughter of the First World War, finally some reappeared through economic necessity during the 1930's Depression. Some changed their form, perhaps growing competitive eg. NW Morris spawning Carnival Morris for girls, and some were "Revived" in a completely new environment. Julian Pilling's collection of postcards of early NW teams showed a high proportion of women's sides which have been largely ignored in more recent historical accounts.

The original "Good Luck" visiting objective was often overlaid with the economic need for the money received, especially in their later years, so that largesse given became a part of the expectation. Several older Cotswold dancers commented that it got like begging. Reinvention in an emasculated form was also a typical Victorian response, reflecting changing attitudes.

5   PERSISTANCE

The evidence from Tudor times is of a nationwide, if limited, use of the morris. The English Reformation that started during Edward VI's reign turned the Church and Civic Authorities against what they saw as a Popish activity well before the growth of the influence of 'Godly People'. It is a fundamental error for morris sides today to imply that Puritans or Oliver Cromwell himself suppressed the morris. James I and Charles I already had to publically encourage performance as a healthy exercise along with archery. The prohibition of maypoles and football matches and the like was because of the risk of social unrest when there was no effective police force and the gatherings of crowds was thought could easily lead to riotous or seditious actions. The morris had collapsed by the time of the Protectorate and the Restoration, emerging again at some stage in various regional forms. For most areas the continuity is unknown, but the urge to perform continued and related activity has been mentioned in many places outside of the what are considered to be the conventional traditional counties.

To the south of the Thames, from east to west, a presumed folk dance desert, there were at least,

a   Lucy Broadwood's last Sussex Morris Man, who dressed in motley, played a trumpet, and danced   fantastically.

b   At Puttenham under the Hog's Back west of Guildford, the morris died because one performer, the captain, insisted that he was to be buried in the only costume. As they were the local carters, they had danced against locals at the pubs in London which they visited,

c   Local references to parties of dancers with fiddlers as musicians visiting houses in Old Farnborough and Old Woking towards the end of the 19th century.

d   The morris at Salisbury which appeared to use the same tune on all its outings but chose a different dance to perform on each occasion. Half the team were always dressed as women.

e   The annual mixed procession at Shaftesbury which was to pay for the town's water supply from a   neighbouring   manor followed by a municipaly funded feast. The Bezant which was the exhibited centrepiece is in the town museum.

f   Simple morris like dances found in the East Somerset mining towns.

The local mummers often included a concluding dance in their show. The Christmas seasonal performance was often because of the hard times that occured when some trades were frozen out and thus the workers unemployed. Just as the NHS and National Insurance killed the need for Friendly Society roles, so did the Benefit System of the Welfare State end the economic incentive to perform traditional customs.

Then there were also known to be Children's Games in many traditional formations including some with chain and wind-up snail movements, rather like the French farandole.

6 EARLIEST EVIDENCE OF THE PERFORMANCE OF SEASONAL PLAYS

What can we learn from other seasonal performances?

Early Medieval mummers were silent performers illustrating the plot being read out by a clerk who was in what looked like the more modern Punch and Judy booth. There is evidence later captured in the English Drama Records of playlets as well as the Corpus Christi Mystery plays. The surviving and collected Robin Hood songs and stories also are suggestive of some robust and probably comic performances, often involving the characters falling into water. Toni Arthur wrote a play for young people which exploited this feature, staged with a plank over a fishpond. The Robin Hood character soon got fed up with changing his costume after each soaking!

But the history of particular idioms does not have to have had to exist for long. The evidence is,

Plough Ceremonies	since	1413
Hero Combat		1730's
Wooing Play		1760
Sword Play		1800

We would like to believe that these were actually more ancient but the trail becomes vaguer and comments are much more generalised further back, and difficult to interpret. However the records of what was performed in the early 16th century before the first appearance of theatres show that the style of production was very comparable to that used for the seasonal plays of later years.

It is thought likely that the widespread texts, which have considerable similarities whereever performed, owe their origins to the versions printed in chap books, the cheaply available reading of common people in the 17th and 18th century. The oldest collected text dates from about 1800. Often plays had local characters as well as the standard ones, and had local references and often local topical asides added, features often ignored by modern revivalists. The characters such as the Quack Doctor did not date back further than the end of the Elizabethan period and the Stuarts. The French and Spaniards were not both enemies until after the Great Armada. The Turkish Knights were once world famous as fighters, being the best trained and equipped in the world until at last bested by an Austrian Prince with superior firepower, for the Ottoman world had turned in on itself rather than continuing to lead technically. This is a potential problem with any centrally controlled economy.

The appearance of a troupe could be deceptive. The late Ted Duckett, a step dancer from Poole, told how his gang dressed up as mummers in paper streamer costumes and then, after formally announcing themselves in the manner of the sword dancers, proceeded to perform their party pieces in turn as did black faced minstrels.

Face colouring is the last vestige of a once common process of "disguising".

Unless it is a full body cover, it does not work to deny identification unless they have never met before which is possible in this day and age, but it is difficult to see how it would in a countryside of small communities with high interdependence. Poachers, like modern commandos, used face painting to avoid being noticed at all. Much more likely it was intended in customs to give the disguiser freedom to behave differently from normal, just as an actor, or as they would say "to free the spirit". It was really for the benefit of the performer. It should be remembered that face colouring, particularly all over, can be frightening, which is why circus clowns have their individual registered patterns of colours, with emphasis on the mouth and eyes.

Full Body Disguise- As with Horses and Bulls, Buryman, Straw Bear, Gullivers, Jack-in-the- Green etc.

False Head- From the Middle Ages and related to what they knew. North Waltham mummers were paid to perform under heads based on medieval mss borders for a film in 1947 called "Uncle Silas"..

Full Face Mask- Tudor period and before, but may have derived from the classical knowledge that arose with the Renaissance, although such are common all over the world.

Eye Mask - As presumed for Highwaymen, then used from Masquerades to Fancy Dress.

Face Painting- Fashionable now with children and sports supporters.

Blacking Up - The 1731 Black Act forbade it, only one morris mention of it before 1750.

Anything recorded as post 1843 is suspect because of the overwhelming influence of black face minstrelsy on all forms of public entertainment in the UK up until World War One. A point now forgotten. Also what other colouring was available then?

This blacking up is often brought up in connection with Border Morris. Eventually someone will take a morris to court over blacking up. It is very desirable that any evidence that it was a common custom, as distinct from an occasional one, is assembled because a barrister will run rings around anyone presenting the currently used arguments.

Much more attention should be given to the European usages of masks as well as the possible significance of the contact with the early and continuing disguising experienced in West Africa.

What were the attitudes to heavily tanned outdoor workers? The Middle and Upper Classes avoided being tanned themselves.

Dark skinned people as soldiers came with the Romans, were met during the Crusades and on medieval and early modern trade routes. Ambassadors and their followers from parts of the Islamic areas were at Queen Elizabeth's court. Blackamoors were exotic personal servants as early as the time of Catherine of Aragon. There were dark skinned Italians and Spanish. King Charles with his quarter Italian blood was known as "Black Boy" and is still commemorated on Inn signs. Later many Iberians were recruited for the south Wales mines in the nineteenth century and, because of their, to the locals, outlandish names, were often renamed Jones.

The Berbers took just seven years to conquer most of Spain, and became known to us as Moors. The English had direct experience of the Moors in Spain, first through academic learning centres with an access to classical writing resources, but also from employment in the Reconquest, and then settling the empty countryside after the ethnic cleansing, and also from trade. The moresque style of textiles and decorations were considered to be the best, and some examples can be seen in the Victoria and Albert museum, but also the Toledo steel as swords and halberds was thought of exceptional quality. Then there were the Barbary Coast Pirates from the Magreb who attacked the West Country and Ireland in the days of James I. From trade with the Levant following the Crusades there was familiarity with the Saracens, then later the Ottoman Turks, but also the exotic peoples, variously known as Ethiopian, Nubian, Nigerian, and even those from the Gold Coast, where the gold bullion for early English coinage was derived via the trans-Saharan caravans. Then the sub-Saharan peoples in West Africa were involved in the three cornered slave trade, which provided the funds to stimulate the start of the Industrial Age in Coalbookdale, and incidentally probably affected the appearance and justifications of some West Country Customs. Trade with the Magreb improved after the Pope excommunicated Queen Elizabeth I!

Black dressed Satans occur in Basque and French/Spanish customs. Black still has negative implications in the West.

Black Faced Minstrelsy existed from the 1840's. So popular was it that by the start of the 20th century it was the most common form of entertainment available in London. After WW1 it became a typical amateur entertainment replacing older traditions, as it depended on performing existing party pieces rather than something especially learnt. But Minstrelsy in the USA promoted a derogatory image of Afro-americans and is now unacceptable.

'Taking offence on behalf of others where none is intended is one of the banes of modern life. Using the criminal law to enforce compliance with the doctrine of diversity is a form of fascism.' Daily Mail p17, 25.03.11.

Colour prejudice in England is reported to have fallen sharply after the abolition of slavery, although this did not happen as quickly as the date of the legislation would suggest, but it was rekindled by the US military stationed in Britain in both World Wars. Their coloured people were given mainly limited pioneer tasks. Did they not recognise that Christ was at least darkish, and that he did not speak in English?

The European experience could be different. "Black Peter" in Holland visits and gives presents on 5th December,

Colour prejudice still existed when I was at school in the late 1940's. An outstanding girl athlete could not gain a place in town or county teams even though she was a fourth generation from the West

Indies, whose grandparents had been well known to my grandfather.

9   THE HARD EVIDENCE

There is much that is not widely known about the 19th century morris. How common were the sides at any one time? What were their catchment areas? How often was there inter-marriage? What else would we like to know? Perhaps decadal maps, or sites of graves. There is still a need to build up more evidence.

Heany and Forrest "Early Morris Annals" is the prime evidence for occurances and mentions of morris up to 1750 in Britain. However quite a few of the references are entries in documents like dictionaries. Forrest's following book is a very good analysis of this evidence. The caution that has got be given is that the earliest references to things with an association with the morris frequently quoted in club brochures prove nothing more than that morris existed somewhere in Europe and that the artifacts were no more than exotic imports, or even that the dancers seen may have been a touring company. William Kemp, Shakespeare's clown, toured Europe with his act, as well as doing and publishing an account of the Nine Days Wonder of a processional form of dance from London to Norwich. The actor Chris Harris has edited and reprinted the account and toured with a one-man performance based on it.

Three Dance Formations have been found in the literature and illustrations of the 16th century. These are the Chain, the Circle, and the going Two by Two, but the morris is often just quoted as performing processionals. The linked chain was the common social dance of the ordinary folk of the time. It is still widely found in Europe in that role from France to Greece. The Circle is of dancers going around a figure standing or dancing separately in the centre. Unfortunately the convention for illustration purposes is to show every dancer doing something different although in practice they all followed the steps of the leader. This pattern is still followed by the Basques in their Sauts where each sequence of steps and capers has its own title which is called and continued until another is chosen. The closest approach in an English dance are the various leapfrog dances in which the dancer at the top perfoms a sequence, each in turn as they circle round, or as in The Rose or similar chorus movements. Going two-by-two, ie in pairs, is the conventional processional which can be for as many pairs as will.

Spanish transmission to North America. Early 1994 there was an exhibition in the Smithsonian in Washington about New Mexico that showed films of the similar morrises and matachins performed in Pueblo Amerindian and Spanish villages in that state. The implements and steps looked culturally dependent but removing these elements what was left was the structure of the common long set dance as found in North Wales, Lancashire. Provence and Northern Italy. The Jesuits had taken the then current Spanish dances to replace the native dances.

In a Penguin book called 'The World Turned Upside Down' there was a reference to Quakers going out like morris dancers. Puzzled, I visited the Quaker library in Birmingham, to be told it was a dig based on the knowledge that preaching Quakers went out in pairs!

The Matachins followed the appearance of the morris as a dance idiom with sticks. It was not so popular.

A frequent mention were the Napkins. Handkerchiefs were invented by King Richard II or III to avoid using the long tails of the sleeves which had been the common practice. Kerchieves or Neckerchiefs were traditionally one yard square before hemming, just the right size to wrap a meal in, etc. The original pocket handkerchief was a quarter of this, eighteen inches square before hemming. This was the size of the morris handkerchief which when held by one corner the other diagonal could reach the ground. The modern pocket handkerchief is only one ninth, that is one foot square before hemming, and a 'ladies' is even smaller!

Records show that before 1800 customs now thought of as common to particular areas actually appeared

instead in different parts of the country. The Cotswold form is deduced to have stretched at least from Bath to Bletchley and presumably to Wootton Bassett and probably further. In the 1740's the famous Bath team was invited to dance during a cricket match in London after it had performed at the Bartholemew Fair

10   INTERNAL EVIDENCE

What can be said about the morris from the evidence from its dances and techniques themselves? The classic morris step, as described by Sharp based on the performance of his oldest informants, needs a reasonably smooth dancing surface. That 'stepping' ended with a 'break', either a plain jump or a more complex cadence is typical of folk step dancing, but not of social dancing at any time, nor is the use of implements such as handkerchiefs. It is not normal for Morris dancers to have any physical contact except for handclapping patterns, whereas 17th century social dancing, at a higher social level, was full of handshaking, kissing and other movements suitable for social situations. The morris does not have progressive figures as with the Assembly Room longways for as many as will, as it is not a form of socialising

The common double step as described by Sharp is not part of the surviving tradition in the 20th century. Riverdance, the Irish exploitation show that is always referenced when considering a major English display, showed dancers always up on the balls of their feet. In light soft shoes this was very morris like. Dancers such as Harry Taylor of Longborough liked to wear special light weight shoes for the morris, even though they could be worn through in a short period of dancing. Country boots were not the preferred footwear! The 19th century English tradition was athletic, a style copied by Sharp's first men's team who had been taken to met traditional dancers. Some of the sources had told Sharp that they learnt and practiced the stepping supported by two chair backs or between the rails of a sheep dip. Ballet dancers have to practice to make their ankle and foot joints strong enough. It is doubtful if traditional dancers of the 19th century had a strength problem, but the modern trend for thinner bones and lighter frames because of the different life style of modern urban based people indicates a potential problem. The classic stepping needs smooth floors, which came into existence about Tudor times. Before that it was threshing floors that were used for social dancing, but hardly for morris. As initially the morris was more of a processional dance, the first morris had to be suitable for typical urban road surfaces, presumably cobbles and the like. In the Middle Ages dancing appears to have been mostly out of doors, which would not have been bowling green smooth. Perhaps this explains the high knee lift in regional styles of stepping.

Other morris steps, for example galleys and capers, have similarities to some used in the galliards and Elizabethan Jigs, but they are far fewer, less elaborate and more economical. Unlike the Basque traditions, it is improbable that the morris contributed to the early development of the professional ballet.

The tunes found in the Cotswold morris are of various ages. Most appear in tune collections but spread over many years. Some such as Trunkles and Shepherd's Hey have not been found and may be ancient. Trunkles might mean Trunk Hose a 17th century fashion for a while. A few are quite late, such as Getting Up Stairs and The Rosetree (in Full Bearing). The former is considered to have been a Black Face Minstrel song first.

The English Country Dance was an upper and middling classes activity that started in the Elizabethan era. No linkage with the dances of the folk has been established. "Country" was from the spirit in which they were danced, and it meant country as in "town and country", where they relaxed and enjoyed themselves. Playford's first edition was published between the time of the battles of Dunbar and Worcester at the end of the Civil Wars with the object of use for dancing at home. Later editions were relevant to the growth of assembly rooms and showed the gradual shift to the more socially appropriate progressive longways-for-as-many-as-will form. The English Country Dance was spread to the continent and many of Europe's preserved folk dances are derivative. It may be necessary to remind that Thomas Hardy wrote that he remembered when he was a teenager the longways dances reaching the servants and country people in Dorset and the Fletts finding a similar spreading of the form into the Highlands and Islands within the living memory of their informants.

The pattern in Playford's first edition for the non-progressive set dances is very suggestive at first sight, but the established source of these social dances was in the theatre and masques. The very limited evidence is for their earlier form being very much simpler. The best conclusion is that social and seasonal dances may have had a common source, but the dance choreographers were far more prolific than the morris.

The standard figures which distinguish the English form of morris from the continental traditions are not those of the Playford dances.

Playford Morris

Up and back a double twice	-	Foot up and down
Siding	-	Half Gyp
Arming	-	Hands Round

and no Cross Over, Back to Back or Rounds as regular movements. Where is the "something and half-hey" repeated pattern which was that which did occur in folk dancing often as a stand along structure?

There is no doubt that the Country dance was popular amongst the middling class, see the endless references in Pepys diaries for their commonality before the rise of the Assembly Rooms developed.

11   HOME GROWN THREADS

When society lived close to a subsistence level, ensuring fertility and a successful harvest could mean the difference between life and death. The technical understanding of farming was until quite late in history based on the writings of the ancients, which was largely empirical and not science based. Also the classical texts were for Mediterranean climes, with their problems of adequate water supply and not those of the northern countries with their issues of enough temperature. It was a problem for the Romans who came to exploit the potential bread basket of the East Midlands and the opposite was found when we settled Australia. The farming practices depended on what appeared to work without knowing why, and there was resistance to any changes because that would be going into the unknown.

The question is therefore what would a real fertility custom consist of? It would not be just a good farming practice but either something which we would call sympathetic magic or an expression of hopes or fears for the current year. Mimicking procedures in a dance or a playlet would be understood by an audience but it does not deserve to be elevated to mean something more. Hitting the ground or capering high and other such Victorian/Edwardian fantasies would be known to be ineffective. But they would allow the performers to express something in terms of things they and their audience knew. Stone age cultures around the world still had hunter gatherer lifestyles as well as primitive farming practices and it was noted by Sachs that it was the men who performed the hunting rituals and the women the planting ones.

We must never underestimate what appears to be primitive cultures. They may lack some sophistication but there are inherently as intelligent as anyone. It has been the folly of West to impose their ill thought through standards.

So what would they have considered? Waiting for the right date or the right weather - such rules are still followed by gardeners, although the justification may be weak. Planting potatoes on Good Friday was one such practice, but even that may have been because it was one day that the gardener could expect to be free to do so. Transhumance, taking the animals up to the higher ground for the summer season worked to the calendar, such as going up on May Day and returning in September/October and having the associated festivities. Harvest Home, Christmas and Shrove Tuesday were traditional feast days to use up the provisions of different limited shelf lives. Killing and preserving surplus livestock that could not be supported through the winter led to having waste that had to be destroyed by burning about the beginning of November. Lent was a recognition that the period before the new crops grew were the starving months anyhow. All such customary activity became frozen into the farming calendar and are still recognised today even though the globalisation has removed the reasons. However the human body has been evolved to suit this old pattern and the current excess supply leads to the modern health problems. The seasonal round in England depends on the local climate, which varied from south to north and from west to east, implying a local view on seasonal customs that had to fit in with the vital survival activities.

The typical date of English Spring customs is not about the time of ploughing, sowing, germination, hoeing, or of lambing and calving, the people would have been too busy. However there was a slack period before starting hay making and harvesting the early crops such as salad leaves after the starving months, thus they were a celebration of apparent success. Unfortunately the past theorists were not gardeners or farmers and did not grasp the realities!

People would use props that they knew - for example heads or skins. There was no guessing at future trends or responding to speculations. There was no historic perspective. Their imagination was limited to what they had or had heard of, for example the largest object known was a ship, so a typical extravagant display was the ship of fools. Is this the origin of the idea of floats? Bobby Wells of Bampton told the story that when trying to explain to locals on his return home from World War One that he had sailed in a liner, the largest object they could think of for comparison was a train.

What sort of Society does the Morris need? - a structured society and seasonal opportunities. But society was always changing, even today pubs are becoming restaurants and potential audiences are more static, and the morris has to struggle to make its impact.

BACK TO THE MIDDLE AGES

12   NATURE OF EVIDENCE

Most of the surviving records are to do with taxation, legal matters, the monarchy, politics and the church. Drama and music development have been exhaustively explored both from the limited evidence and from their early links with religious expression. Relevant surviving illustrations are often peripheral to other sources, such as mss margins, church wall paintings, stone and wood carvings, or incidentally in the use of contemporary images in what were intended as historical religious statements. Going far enough back in time there were the cave wall paintings. Interpretation involves degrees of extrapolation backwards of lessening credibility as the time gap increases.

The quantity of evidence surviving reduces the further back in time, both through natural losses, smaller populations, lower literacy and less complex life styles. The recording was less mature earlier, caring about fewer matters, and reading was more cumbersome and limited in numbers before printing existed. The interests were simpler and the spin placed on matters was coarser or more blatant, and the sense of historical accuracy much weaker. Often material is only found as complaints by the Church yet its consequent pronouncements, usually negative, were often ignored, which adds to the confusion. Unfortunately, also some things were thought to be too commonplace to be remarked upon at all.

13 CAN WE TRUST MODERN INTERPRETATION OF HISTORICAL EVIDENCE?

We cannot believe all the judgements of past publications; the available accessible material has often been skimmed over and views formed without a true regard for the evidence and reliance has often been placed on material from hostile sources. An example is the reputation of the Duke of Monmouth, for whom the evidence is derived mostly from James II, who was a superb dancer, along with his wife, just as were some of Queen Elizabeth's courtiers, and this skill has never appealed to academic writers. For generations senior figures excelled at war fighting until Tudor times when the emphasis at court changed to the social graces. Another example is Richard Cromwell, the son of Oliver, who was anything but Tumble-Down-Dick, but losers do not write history!

Three things are hard to explore through archaeology, music. dance and trade, as they leave so little evidence. A consequence is that explanations of remains have tended to be in terms of ritual and religion, which even if appropriate, probably only applied to the later periods. A map of megalithic monument remains across Europe, which although they varied in form from area to area, shows that they were never a great distance from the sea, infering that the underlying culture was probably a sea going one. Trade is evidenced from the wide distribution of items from tracable sources, such as hand axes from the Lake District. Local markets and seasonal Fairs have been evident from the earliest of records and should be assumed to have had even earlier origins. Both buyers and sellers need to know where and when to meet, hence the likelihood of fixed sites and dates for business of necessity related to astronomical calendar observations. However I doubt if these were held on the observable astronomical dates as it would seem unlikely that people would hang around at sites waiting for these to occur but would expect notification of it being held some days after the required observation had been made. It is unreasonable for actual fairs to occur on the same day everywhere as barterers/traders/sellers would have to be able to travel!

Another concern is that we were very dependent on particular sources such as Bede's history of early Britain, which was written many years after the events and for a king who needed to be impressed. For a long while we have believed that England was aggressively invaded by waves of Saxons, Angles and Jutes, but there is little archaeological evidence of the associated expected damage or slaughter. The Saxon shore forts were probably more like trading posts for dealing with the new vibrant and stimulating cultures which were far from the ignorant impoverished barbarians of classical literature. The DNA evidence shows a gradual shift from Saxon to British genes going from east to west across the country which is hardly compatible with ethnic cleansing.

History can be manufactured by stringing together disconnected facts. Do you believe that the Chinese in 1423 sailed the world with a huge fleet and mapped the Americas, and in 1431 again sailed this time to Florence to share their encyclopaedic knowledge and initiate the Renaissance? Did Columbus and Magellan have maps of where they were going when sailing into the supposed unknown. Did a tsunami wipe out Chinese settlements all around the Pacific? Did this cause the Chinese Emperor to reverse the country's policy towards the outer world for centuries?

The common theme was fund raising at a time when the tithes were for the support of the clergy, not for the building. Local aristocracy, guilds and perhaps incumbents did take responsibility for the upkeep of parts bug it was seldom enough so they were dependent on what could be raised. Thus the Games, which were like modern fetes with games, sports, competitions, food and drink, produce stalls and also organised entertainments. These varied over the years as fashions changed.

Church Ales were very common, after all there were eventually 10,000 parish churches. In the days when brewing was a very local and a mainly household task, the church wardens would organise a special brew, presumably stronger than normal, which as sold to lubricate the celebration of a local saint's day or the feast of dedication.

Organised entertainments would circulate around the neighbouring fetes. Such Ales would include the local expressions of the-world-turned-upside-down and other disrespectful behaviours. There were no police other than the parish constable and hence this behaviour was traditional with the licence that went with fools and clowns. The other names used did not represent much difference. The King Games - much of which were things to take the mickey about. The May Games - with a King and Queen, or Lord and Lady in charge, and also the Robin Hood Games - with little overlap in time with morris or Maid Marian and the stories allowing many opportunities for horseplay.

Early Drama Records - to be completed and then consequently studied. We need a current list of those volumes already published and the other in progress items. For example Hampshire is finished but due for publication and Gloucestershire is in work. These collectively should cover the period of the break up of the Middle Ages following the Black Death and the changes to society and the concurrent growth of secular entertainments. The booket on Hampshire shows what is considered to be a typical history of the developments.

15   ANTECEDENTS

The English centric view of history is not helpful. We need to recognise our standing with other kingdoms over the early years, where the ideas originated and what was genuinely indigenous. Until the Tudors we were probably a backwater, a lagging developing country clearly being influenced by the outside world. Think colonies becoming dominions and no greatness until Elizabethan times and the rise of an effective navy.

Morris did not appear out of the blue. There are references to morris abroad before those in England. There are

possible sources of importation.

Queens were brought in for dynastic reasons from various countries. They usually brought with them native courtiers and servants. Note the tender ages of most of them and their evident need for support in a strange land. It requires a map to show where some of these places were.

Kings and Wives

Henry II

Life 1133-1189 Reign 1154-1189
Eleanor of Aquitaine   1122-1204
Married 1152 Age 30
b o/l

Richard I   (Lionheart)

Life 1157-1199 Reign 1189-1199
Berengaria of Navarre   1165-1230
Married 1191 Age 26   o/l

John I   (Lackland)

Life 1167-1216 Reign 1199-1216
Isabella of Angoulême   1186-1246
Married 1200 Age 14   o/l

Henry III

Life 1207-1272   Reign 1216-1272
Eleanor of Provence   1222-1291
Married 1236 Age 14   o/l

Edward I

Life 1239-1307 Reign 1272-1307
Eleanor of Castile   1244-1290
Married 1254 Age 10 b
Marguerite of France   1282-1317
Married 1298   Age 16   o/l

Edward II

Life 1284-1327   Reign 1307-1327
Isabella of France   1292-1358
Married 1304 age   12 b o/l

Edward III

Life 1312-1377   Reign 1327-1377
Philippa of Hainault   1314-1369
Married 1328 Age   14

Richard II

Life 1367-1400 Reign 1377-1399
Anne of Bohemia   1366-1394
Married 1382 age   15
Isabella of Valois   1387-1410
Married 1395 age   8   o/l

Henry IV

Life 1367-1413 Reign 1399-1413
Mary de Bohun 1369-1394
Married 1382 Age 13 b
Joan of Navarre 1370-1437
Married 1403 Age   33   o/l

Henry V

Life 1387-1422 Reign 1413-1422
Catherine of Valois   1401-1437
Married 1420 Age 19   o/l

Henry VI

Life 1421-1471 Reign 1422-1461,
Margaret of Anjou   1430-1482
Married 1445 Age   15   o/l

Edward IV

Life 1442-1483 Reign 1461-1470,
Elizabeth Woodville   1437-1492
Married 1461   Age 24   o/l

Edward V

Life 1470-1483 Reign   1483
Unmarried

Richard III

Life 1452-1485   Reign 1483-1485
Anne of Warwick   1456-1485
Married 1472 Age 16 b

b = king married before reigning,

o/l = queen outlived the king,

rem = queen remarried after king's death.

There are only three in this period who were mature at marriage. Berengaria never set foot in England. Eleanor of Aquitaine had a very turbulent life, although from the home of the troubadours, she and her husband did not get on, and she spent 15 years imprisoned. That leaves Joan of Navarre who is of the same period as the Black Prince and John of Gaunt who invaded Spain.

As late as 2008 a book stated,

'This most peculiar of English country traditions seems to be a hand-me-down from an altogether more lethal and martial ritual brought home by John of Gaunt (1340-99). His Spanish expeditions brought him into conflict with the Moors, who impressed him with their hyper-violent sword-dance in which those who lost the rhythm could well lose their head to boot. Public demonstrations of Morrish dancing caused the ritual to move into English rural tradition as Morris dancing, in which the dancers wore black makeup and the swords were replaced with wooden ones reflected in the little stick that dancers "fence" with today.'

Amazingly this was repeated on BBC's Radio Gardeners Question Time at the beginning of April 2011!

The classic account, eg. Young's "History of British Music" (1967), has, 'in 1381 John of Gaunt set up a Court of Minstrels at Tutbury in Staffordshire, which presided over by an elected King, was allowed to exercise authority over all of the craft in five of the midland counties. Five years later John of Gaunt brought back from Spain a troupe of Moorish dancers and the combination of their practices with those proper to the traditional English Fool's Dance is said to have provided the basis for the Morris Dance. It was in honour of John of Gaunt, therefore, that the Robin Hood and Morris dancers continued to wear his emblem - of three ostrich feathers - and the Red Lion on his shield after his marriage with Constance of Castile provided the name of inns which were for centuries the starting point for ceremonial May Day dances'. Note there is more to it than moors.

But what is the source of this story ? The early morris records do not talk of sticks or of makeup. There is a gap of a century to explain as well. Is there any historical account of the development of Spanish dances to give a clue? The Baques recognise that there were Spanish dances with similar titles to theirs but naturally do not accept that theirs have any debt to them.

It would seem that it was the uncharacteristic expensive celebrations by Henry VII for the arrival of Catherine of Aragon that triggered the first appearances of the morris in its 16th century role. That court dances were not common to different countries was found when the princes met Catherine at Dogmersfield House in north east Hampshire on her way up to London. When they tried to dance together it was found to be impossible because of their quite different interpretations of the court dances, so each party had to dance with their own people.

The European wide contacts must not be underestimated. Besides trade which perhaps did not involve a large number of people outside of the wool export business, there were the many contacts through the churches. It is unlikely that the monasteries were involved but there were many church councils, of which the Council of Constance was of major importance and that brought leading prelates together for many months with their entertainments organised by the various attending groups as part of their public relations campaigns.

A   THE CHURCH

The analysis of surviving Church Warden Accounts covering fund raising and its costs shows that it is not clear what entries mean, therefore it is unknown whether if the entertainments are local or brought in. The cost of kit was such that some places had to borrow kit and equipment. The reading of entries has to take into account the analysis of changes in language and in the topics covered. The Renaissance brought in new jargon, and the use of drama to illustrate issues, there was the impact of printing and the consequences of the availability of bibles in native tongues. These changes in attitudes were important.

The role of senior church prelates was altering with a switch to role of being more of a Civil Service. This was because the church was the only source of trained bureaucrats who were not soldiers. It had an effect on how the church responded to what was happening in society. We see the Church as opposed to festive culture, a Protestant view from Edward VI's time. But the attitude persists. A few years ago when invited to dance at a church fete held in the churchyard at Silchester, the Abercorn Stave dancers were asked to dance in the track outside as they were not quite sure about the propriety.

England lagged Italy by up to two centuries. The link of "folk" behaviour to medieval practices recognised as early as 1725.

B   MIDDLE AGES

This was a period of New Technologies - some western, some eastern - making the first Industrial revolution, from spinning wheels and wind mills to, mining. There was a fully developed religious life, which accumulated riches, partly from exploitation of the wildernesses, with varieties of Monks, Friars, and finally the

Jesuits. There were the massive buildings which were impressive. The Normans rebuilt in stone replacing the Saxon Crosses and Minsters. The decorative and performing arts gradually flourished with the urge for only the best for God, leading to a taste for extravagance, as can still be seen in the decoration in Catholic churches abroad

The period led to the concept of nations with the associated need for loyalty and emphasis on prestige forms. But Europe was always fighting with itself.

It was also the period of the development of privacy and commerce, buildings had separate rooms. Trade grew with far waay places such as the Levant and the Magreb.

The Black Death , which had struck before in the 6th century,as well as the 14th, killed half the population and led to a major cultural shift

C   THE GUILDS

The Primary objective of the early Merchant or Trade Guilds persisting until quite late was religious observances and only secondary was trade regulation. Their activities included processionals dressing up in expensive liveries, if one existed, not only on their own days but is support of other organisations, to show their status and to emphasise their prestige. They paid   for musicians and no doubt in due course for morris. Funds were needed and raised through various procedures, as such displays also needed patronage. The guilds like the monasteries were obvious targets for Henry VIII. The selling of the properties led to the great rebuilding of the countryside, the redistribution of wealth, the glories of the Elizabethan age and eventually to a civil war.

D   BEFORE ALL THIS - THE PAGANS

The Dark Ages have become better understood over the last 50 years. We are no longer dependent on biased documents produced long after the events. Survivals from that period would have been wider spread than traces of traditions would suggest. The Christian Faith dominated life from the time of St Boniface. England was thoroughly catholic and the most catholic in Europe before the Reformation. This has the biggest impact on activities that require community approval or participation.

The Church, particularly the monasteries, led with the dramatization of services, the introduction of Mystery Plays, the painted walls, the stained-glass windows, and the illustrations in stone and in mss, all intended to educate and inform.

E   WICCA

This is a modern phenomena with no continuity with pagan times. There are no historical statements suggesting Morris was ever involved although the Pagan Times has listings of modern Morris Events!

Magic is basically a delusion, dependent on unsupportable unscientific ideas, e.g.. Homeopathy, alternative medicine and placebos. It assumes Sympathetic Magic exists and this opens up another discussion area outside of this paper.

However it involves a good caring and living style, see the book by Prof Hutton of Bristol.

17   RECOGNISING THE AGES OF THE MORRIS

Prestige Age - in the initial phase, essentially the 16th century, the morris appeared in prestige events. Sponsored locally by the church and civic authorities with expensive costumes. Alternatively, it was done by professional player touring companies who offered plays, triumphal entries, interludes and the morris. One must be beware of assuming that local references to some aspect of the morris, such as the purchase of bells, refers to a locally recruited team. The evidence of who actually did the morris dances in this period is very sparse, but some sources suggest it was yeomen rather than those of lower social status. Status was defined in terms of annual value of property and land owned. With the death of Henry VIII, the administration of Edward VI started a full scale move to Protestantism and the reduction or elimination of anything considered Popish. This naturally included the prestige morris.

Luther approved of dancing, Calvin did not. The English Independents (Congregationalists) did the Presbyterians did not. The modern United Reformed Church is the modern combination of the two, but it is no longer an issue since the Victorians had their way..

There was a gap through the 17th century with all its social upheavals and endless rethinking.

Heyday Age - the 18th century - Following the Restoration of Charles II there was some return to Merrie England with maypoles, bonfires and other seasonal behaviours. But not exactly as before as attitudes had developed with the new generations. Through the 18th century the morris appears to have flourished but not in its first form. This is the period of the good luck visit, for which the recipient uses the opportunity to practice their philanthropy, from

May Garlands carried by children to Bringing in the May by adults, to the morris and mummers and the various touring hobby animals.

Decline Age - the 19th century - The licence of the 18th century with its drunken behaviour and crudities and the habit of St Monday were counter-productive to the growing need for economic effort to support the Agricultural and Industrial developments of the time. Production needed a disciplined workforce. The objective of cultured society was to establish rational recreations, codification of sports, a woman's proper place, and a woman's customary wage, a straight jacket that still bedevils today.

Revival Age - the first half of the 20th century - The artistic merit inherent in folk culture, in song, music and dance, began to be appreciated at the end of the 19th century. Societies were founded, lectures given and displays and concerts organised. The activities of the Esperance Club sparked off an enthusiasm rapidly spreading to all the counties. This was interrupted by World War One. After the war it became an activity formed by Middle Class attitudes, descriptions fixed, clubs, classes, standards set and displays arranged. There was seen to be a need to have men involved and there was a slow growth in one sex teams, the discovery of touring, and the realisation that memories could still be tapped. The invention of squire and bagman, ales, feasts and instructionals.

Reinvention Age - the second half of the 20th century - The discovery of the morris by the people who benefited from the growth in education after the war and who came from families who could have been the heirs of the traditions. The growth in interest in local things.

18   CONCLUSIONS

a   All of today's Morris has been "Reinvented"

b   What is preserved from the 19th century morris is unknowable in the detail actually required, because of the limitations of the available notations.

c   The old morris forms predate modern sports, all of which were codified in the 19th century, as part of the urge for rational recreation.

d   Most forms are linked to simple Country Dance forms, or elements but with no repetitive progressions, nor quadrilles or waltzes.

e   The Tudor Morris would probably be unrecognisable today, perhaps only Abbots Bromley.

f   Opportunities for the first Morris events grew out of the changes from the medieval to the early modern world.

g   A huge time gap of nearly 1000 years still exists to get back to truely pagan times.

h   Superficial similarities in costume, although intriguing, are no guide to choreography. Illustrations, Maps and references have to be added.

To begin to understand the morris it has to be recognised that people have a need for leisure and that humans in a crowd have an in built desire for festive behaviour involving music, dance, dressing up and sharing food and drink. It can be seen today at sports fixtures where people go to participate rather than watch and even in political demonstrations of processions and picketing.

That is not the belief of all. Our Civil War divided the country between those who wanted a festive culture and those who did not. The Protestant work ethic was responsible for the eminence of the country through the 18th and 19th centuries.

ANNEX

THE RECOGNISED HISTORICAL AGES
Terms in common use.

Black Death

Renaissance

Reformation

    Abolition of the Monastries

    The Great Rebuilding

Early Modern

    Civil Wars

    Restoration

    Dutch Invasion (Glorious Revolution) & new technologies

Enlightenment

    Agricultural and Industrial Revolutions

    Georgian

    Regency

    Revolutionary and Napoleonic wars

Modern

    Victorian

    Edwardian

    First World War

    Depression

Post Modern

file : morris01.wri

DO-IT-YOURSELF

This is the personal aspect of dance-leadership supplementing the information contained in pamphlet No 1 'Handing-On' compiled by Douglas and Helen Kennedy and published by the EFDSS. The authors are unkniown now but the style is that of Douglas. It is intended as a Guide to enable folk dance leaders to tune up their natural dance technique. This personal aspect of leadership was omitted from the pamphlet 'Handing-On' as not everyone need be interested in the inner secrets of folk dance action. The language suggests it was written by Douglas Kennedy.

This guide is not only to help the leaders to help themselves, but with the hope that their increased effectiveness will improve folk dance technique generally. The leader must be careful not to 'teach' this 'tuning up' directly to his pupils. He or she should keep the 'inside' knowledge as the leader's asset which is at the back not in the front of his mind when presenting dances. He must aim always at giving the best picture of the dance for this visual picture is the leader's most potent 'medicine', remembering that the average folk dancer, as with the general run of ballroom dancers, is content at first with his own standard of performance, mediocre as it may be.

The observations that follow are based upon our appreciation of traditional processes and methods in folk music, song and all types of folk dance. These always reflect a whole-heartedness and utter absorption in the expression. Nothing is done just for effect or in the pursuit of some aspect of beauty, but everything is concentrated on living the part. Beauty is undisputably present in the easy sureness of performance in the economy of action and the dignity of bearing that accompanies true skill, but above all in having something important to say and saying it with complete sincerity.

Folk dancing is something more than just walking about to traditional dance music, but it must be built upon the basis of everyday human action and must preserve that naturalness. The word 'dancing' calls up a vista of moving particles, and as applied to a person one pictures sparkling eyes, a buoyant air, with the body 'lit up' and all the particles in a state of excitement. This condition one sees in native primitive dancing and in some folk dancing, but for a large proportion of folk dancers in England the chief satisfaction seems regrettably to be limited to mastering the unusually rich variety of figures and patterns. It is only the few who get 'lit up' and sparkle. 'Sparkle' is a quality that seems to have been gradually declining with the march of civilisation. No doubt this quality and other 'folk' qualities of dance have been better preserved among the country folk themselves by the conditions of rural life, with its calls upon bodily vigour and its education of bodily skills and dexterities. Can these disappearing qualities which are associated with the folk tradition be recaptured even in the all-pervading urban outlook and circumstances of today? We suggest that the remedy lies to hand in the recreative properties of the dance itself. These include the youthful energies which constantly seek outlet and appear as jive, rock and roll, and other forms of relatively unbridled rhythmic dancing practiced by our young people today. These energies can be harnessed and guided through folk dance channels to increase enjoyment and improve performance. Folk dancing when 'lit up' is completely infectious, prompting onlookers to join in.

From long experience we are convinced that this infectious element of 'good dancing' is best transmitted through the visual picture of dancers in action. Such transmission has always been the traditional method of passing on style and character in performance from generation to generation. In these days of ubiquitous TV, presentation by the visual method is as readily acceptable and more appropriate than ever. Verbal descriptions of dance-action by themselves are quite inadequate, and any talk about folk dances can't describe much more than the form, where you go, which way you come back, and practically nothing about what is happening to you while in transit. This internal happening the leader and teacher must know about and be able to show vividly by dramatising his own actions. Therefore his own dance action must be as good as possible and look robust, yet effortless, rhythmic and fluent, still keeping his own personal idiom.

Our aim here is to prompt the individual leader to conduct his own self-analysis and try and do his own tuning. He can improve the tuning of his instrument, his own body, to speak with such effectiveness that a dance group, observing him demonstrate dance action, gets the right idea of its style and character more or less unconsciously. He must clearly remember that this analysis is a private examination of himself and we repeat that he must not inflict directly this inner knowledge upon his group.

Alongside his own infectious dancing he must of course see to the other requirements that affect the responses of the group. Congenial surroundings, persuasive music, relaxed atmosphere of enjoyment and a gay light-handed touch, all help to free the passages for dance impulse. It is not, however, sufficient to place the onus wholly upon the music, which after all is only a part of the the basis of dance expression.

Passing on dance quality by infection can be done in a number of ways. In the case of Morris and Sword Dancing, when the leader often is dealing with a set at a time, his own performance within the set is his best method of tutoring. In the larger social dance gatherings he has to 'dramatise' the qualities in the picture so that the infection can reach further out into the whole company. He will be all the more effective if he can find ways of making his own music, or even just rhythmic sounds, to match his movements. For one thing, this enables him to show action 'in slow motion', an essential aspect of his visual picture of the dance.

The self-analysis which is recommended should be made by the leader in private, and when practising he should recollect that he is not really a soloist, for his actions must be shaped to fit his partner and be related to the movements of other couples in the set.

"Do-It-Yourself" may be conveniently summarised under four technical sections which we will develop in more detail later. These are :

1. Wholeself (Holism)

The whole person is involved in actions, whether small scale or large scale, with the power of the whole body behind them.

2. Float on Air with Propulsion

The propulsion of a buoyant, elevated and air conscious body.

3. Feeling Ahead

The bodily skill which depends on anticipation of movement (feeling the next action in advance).

4. Joining in, or Participation

The spread of infection from part to part in the body, from partner to partner and to others in the dance, and ultimately to whet the appetite of onlookers to join in and be part of it.

THE BASIS OF ANALYSIS

1.   Wholeself (Holism)

The dancer's instrument is his whole person, body and soul. All of it must not only be able to 'speak' but the action, large or small, must spring from the centre. As an old Morris Dancer had it, "It isn't the legs as does the dancing - it's the 'hitch-up' of the body". The hitch is not just a physical lift. With that goes the inner lift - the sense of elation. This wholesale character in folk dance movement is not unfortunately as general as it should be. Too much of what we see is leg action and even that is confined to motion from the knees downward. Coupled with this restricted gait goes the discouraged posture of downcast head, sagging shoulders and lack-lustre expression. Such prim, half-hearted movement is the very antithesis of folk dance tradition. 'Dancing' implies the participation of all bodily particles in an animated exercise. So long as all parts of the person are capable of taking a share not all parts need be equally involved. But the feeling of animation must pervade all parts. Even when action is limited to a minor gesture, such as a laugh, a wink, a handshake or a clap, the gesture, to be expressive must be warmed by the participation of the whole person, who is then 'putting his heart into it'.

2.   Float on Air with Propulsion

The 'natural' dancer (and the well trained one) works from high level and descends from that level to brush the ground lightly or powerfully with rhythmic step tracery. He knows that he has to be up before he comes down to register his footfall with the beat. The layman's false picture, very prevalent, is that he must launch himself up with the beat instead of landing down with it.

With a buoyant carriage not only are the legs freed for wholesale action, but the 'hitch-up' enables the supporting foot to start its drive with a comparatively weightless body already on its way. The pulsation spreads from the body centre out to the extremities undulating through the joints to the feet. Freed from the usual 'daily' burden, the body at once gains a new sense of poise. The head, balanced sensitively, also ceases to be a burden, and immensely heavy as it is, now helps to guide and control the bodily action, giving it added power if need be. Meanwhile, shoulders, neck and arms all share in this more skilful balancing act and each part learns to carry its own weight. A dancer so elevated and poised finds a new and almost cat-like facility of movement.

The good dancer is also more conscious of the air, the medium in which he moves, just as a swimmer entrusts himself to tangible water, and treats it as a friend, rather than as a foe to be brushed aside, so the buoyant and elevated dancer moving more above the surface of the ground, gets some support from his more tenuous medium. The higher ceiling in which the dancer "floats" gives him the scope to drop to ground level with steps of strength or tenderness according to mood. Moreover there is within the dancer a ballooning faculty enabling him to rebound back into his air ceiling. This ballooning gives the appearance of effortlessness so characteristic of all fine dance action. To launch his person into the air and to keep himself on the rebound requires the skilful propelling movement of the supporting foot, a fact which is often not understood. Next we need to encourage the fullest scope of leg action so that the thighs as well as the lower part of the leg participate. Mountain folk habituated to walking uphill are noted for the full scope and buoyancy of their step. Those who live in flat countries, and even more, the city dwellers, are content with a restricted action, from the knee downwards, particularly noticeable among women.

3. Feeling Ahead

It takes an appreciable time for a feeling of movement to reach from the centre to the extremities. A slap in the face, to be dramatic, depends on the build-up of emotion that triggers off the act of slapping, the 'flow' of the slap proceeds with a growing crescendo that reaches its climax with an effect that is all the more remarkable for its delay and because by this time it is expected. The sensitive mover can anticipate each movement through the faculty of knowing what his body is going to do before he acts. Knowing the feeling, he can even safely leap before he looks. By comparison with such anticipation your quick 'thinker' is slow. This impulse of anticipated movement, so characteristic of all animal life, is in us in danger of becoming extinct, a fact most noticeable in folk dancing. As grown-ups we learn to stop and think. When we apply this attitude to such a primeval act as dancing we develop anxieties as to details of our dance journey and can't enjoy the travel. Dance, as children know very well, is an enjoyable adventure in expression and they relish every particle of motion on the way. This old enjoyment of our early ancestry has to be regenerated as an essential part of dance experience. 'Knowing' beforehand what a movement feels like becomes largely a matter of practice and experience. With the growing knack, one recovers also the sharper sense of rhythm and the combined skill shows up in a noticeable absence of effort. Traditional folk dancers never appear to be grappling with a difficulty. Rather they look as if something was gripping them. This picture of easy effortlessness is rather different from the view prevalent today of dance as a synchronisation of a piece of movement with a measured piece of music, and showing as a concentration of willpower to keep the action in time. Such effort in fact is ill-timed, for it wastes energy instead of conserving it, being against rather than with the waves of rhythm. The dancer then, instead of being lifted and thrilled by the waves, fights for his passage.

4. Joining in, or Participation

Participation in dance is another of the primeval sensibilities tending to wither under the stresses of modern life. The all-pervading warmth or elation felt by the animated dancer should be not only shared with his partner, but also with the company that composes the dance set. Such a sharing of 'life' within the dance set increases the depth of participation which then becomes strong enough to melt the crust of any shy and self-conscious ones who find it so hard to forget themselves when just on their own. In the exchange of moods with others in lively participation the shyer ones find loss of self a surprisingly easy matter. Such dance experiences are commonplace, but even so they often exceed all expectations, for the powers and energies that can be unleashed in dance participation can be prodigious. It is the harnessing of these energies that produces real team-work. This energy of expression, when set free, refreshes, and recreates not only the dancers themselves, but it affects the musicians, and they in turn are stirred to new inspiration. The effect on the onlooker is to prompt him to join in and it is this compulsion that accounts for the tenacity of the folk dance and which has kept it alive in a world that has in other respects grown far away from country life and country custom.

The ritual folk dances - the Morris and the Sword dances - without this effect on the onlooker, become meaningless exercises.

DO IT YOURSELF - A catechism for the leader to test himself

We have set out this more detailed analysis in the form of common failings (which produce a mediocre standard of performance) together with certain questions to test existing levels of performance with a view to improvement.

The Body as a complete dance instrument

If any part of the body is 'left out in the cold' and does not participate it may well be a hinderance to the full expression of dance, which always comes from the body centre.

(Common failings : Actions confined to legs and feet. Not using the complete limbs, limiting arm actions to forearm and hands, (eg.clapping), limiting leg action to the part from the knees downward. Restricted movement is often due to anxiety or doubt of ability to cope with forms and patterns and to get these completed in the requisite time)

1.   Do you feel your dancing increases your animation?

2.   Do you start all your movements with an actual swing of the body or with the sense of body weight?

3.   Can you 'track' flow of movement from the centre outwards? Does your movement flow right out through thigh to foot and through shoulders and arms to hands?

Buoyant carriage takes the weight off the feet.

Elevated poise 'lifts' the level and helps to keep the body alive and relieves feet of their burden.

(Common failings : Passive carriage, bent head, lifeless arms, lack-lustre eyes and a generally sagging aspect often 'gone' at the knees)

1.   Can you extend your body without exaggerating and thus starting the sense of lift and relieving weight   from legs? (Egg out of egg-cup)

2.	Do you habitually look out at eye level or do you feel it safer to watch the ground?

3.	Are your arms passengers? Can you use them (carry them) so that they help buoyancy without being flamboyant?

Air-borne and Air-conscious.

The air is friendly to the 'good dancer' as water is to the good swimmer. It is not to be ignored or regarded as an obstruction to be thrust aside.

(Common failings: If the dancer fails to 'breast it' and 'float' he tends to bob up and down and drop like a stone 'denting' the floor surface when he seeks to be forceful. Without the power of delayed approach, he misses the pleasure of 'poetry in motion')

1.   Are you conscious when moving?

2.   Can you reach your high level in time to drop onto the first footfall?

3.   Can you do this for instance in the Schottishe step with continuity in the alighting, or are you content   to take a step and hop, soon tiring?

4.   Do you know how to delay this drop-on-to-ground in dancing to gain expressiveness - like swearing - Bl...ast! or for a tender approach, like placing the best teacup on the shelf?

5.   Is you body poised above the working leg and foot, so exercising control for lightness and power?

6.   Can you vary your dance passage in speed and strength so that your motion 'talks' (intelligently) in phrases?

Propulsion

Positive 'drive' is needed for the initial impulse and for continued motion - like a guided missile. This drive comes directly from the supporting foot. The dance-walk step calls for this conscious propulsion, more forceful in the American Western-style of square dancing. There is more time to give zest to the step and propulsion in the Hornpipe rhythm than there is in the fast Reels and Jigs.

(Common failings: The failing of putting out a foot to take a step, the body trailing after with no propulsion)

1.   Can you transfer your walk into expressive dance with a chuckle before each footfall?

2.   The 'Pas de Basque' step is the essence of propulsion. Can you propel yourself off your stationary foot, from rest?

3.   Are you conscious of the two beats in the 'Rant' step and can you vary the emphasis to suit North Country and South Country dances?

4.   In all the double steps, can you give added expression to the second pulse?

5.   Are you satisfied that you invariably propel yourself into dance and keep moving with propulsion?

Feeling Ahead

Dancers must 'feel' before they leap ; as the eye in reading is in advance of the utterance, so the 'sense' of dance gesture is ahead of the action.

Common failings : The inexperienced dancer almost invariably seeks to coincide his dance step with the metrical beat. For true dance movement this is too late, the time for expression being expired before the feeling of it has begun)

1.   Does your body 'know' the action that lies ahead in every movement?

2.   In clapping do you anticipate the climax of the handclap and give it feeling and meaning, or do you aim to coincide the clap with the pulse, which usually has the effect of hurrying the rhythm?

3.   When dealing with a partner can you (as the man) give your partner the warning sense of anticipation and confidence in movements such as Promenade and other forms of leading?

4.   Can you also give anticipatory warning in turns and spins?

5.   Can you (as the woman) be ready to follow and give the necessary weight and momentum? But not too ready!

6.   In the pivot swing, can you anticipate and rotate head, shoulders and upper body smoothly round, making partner share this feeling before you move off the propelling foot?

7.   Have you had waltz trouble, which usually arises from the lack of feeling of anticipation? Can you   again rotate your shoulders and those of your partner with the anticipated pressure off your supporting foot before taking the sequence of waltz steps which, when started correctly, tend to take care of themselves?

Participation and Teamwork

In the folk dances the teamwork grows out of the human actions of individuals infecting each other, stimulating them all to a higher level of performance. The absorption in the shared experience does not mean coming down to a common level, but on the contrary, unleashes a new source of hitherto untapped energy (as in various forms of sport).

(Common failings: restricting expression by conforming to a common drill - dressing straight lines etc instead of expanding into the surge of the communal rhythm)

1.   Do you share your rhythm with the rest of the team?

2.   Do you enjoy the sense of sharing movements with your partner in a country dance, or do you isolate   yourself?

NOTE : The guidance given above is directed at social folk dancing in the true folk dance tradition, based on the relationship of man and partner. In England however the dances have also been widely used in children's and adult education, where dancers are frequently of one sex. Nevertheless, our advice in general applies also to leadership in these fields. Our written descriptions may read with a cold-blooded effect, but they must not be allowed to discourage the light-hearted amateur. Technique should be taken with a grain of salt, for it is essential that the leader, at all costs, preserves his own light-heartedness and the sense of fun inherent in the social folk dance.

Finally it must be again emphasized that this guidance is only for personal use and that the leader should never endeavour to impart it directly on social occasions.

MORRIS BASICS WORKSHOP & BEGINNERS

WHY

The origin of this material was a workshop for morris beginners at Sidmouth. The time available was naturally insufficient to produce good dancing, but it did allow of explaining what they were trying to achieve. This note is intended as the basis of a group workshop or a solo workout in which dancers try the movements as they are discussed, in order to appreciate the points being examined. The vision is of a lively and energetic dance.

To the "Experienced" Leader - If you do not work explicitly on "dance" technique yourself or perhaps are not even sure what this means, then you may not be as well equipped to teach others as you think, and you may be passing on bad practices and even creating confusion. It is a potential handicap for a foreman not to be aware of the objectives, emphases, stresses and timings in movement, and to be entirely dependent on just "showing".

The normal club environment approach to beginners takes two or three years to develop into a proficient Cotswold dancer, but more effective training methods based on a greater understanding of what to do could speed this up. But in parallel to the training, as in many sports, some degree of fitness has also to be developed.

Remember that the ultimate objective for the dancers is to participate in the morris being performed in public.

Beginners - Other dance specialities explain the whys and wherefores of their technique to participants, but this is seldom so in the English folk dance world. The "traditional process" is claimed, but it supposes that locally there exist enough good dancers on which to model. Although it can and has worked as a club policy, it is risky and it is often used as an easy option or as a cloak for inexperience or, at worst, ignorance.

The first problem for a teacher is seeing what is being taught from the beginners point of view. The training needs to have exercises that give the beginner a vocabulary of actions and words to which they can relate their attempts at the movements, even though the final objective is a seamless flow through a musical phrase.

It is often forgotten by the more experienced dancer that beginners have a problem with the jargon, and with both the observation and perception of movements, and after a while they do not remember what they have been shown without some reinforcement, for example by extra description or explanation. In particular they are confused by the unspoken differences between nominally similar movements within dances, let alone those between "traditions".

Cotswold Morris is not disciplined in the same manner as the North West Morris - its characteristic allows personal expression through the dance movements. The beginner needs to be helped both to develop a mix of body control, called motor skills, and expression through action, and to learn the techniques of recognising and remembering movement sequences.

We can only learn "what-we-almost-know", therefore we must build on from existing experience, learning and adding one thing at a time, trying to build up relevant movement habits, not just by saying it once, but through using sequences that can reinforce memories by acting as a continual reminder.

Stresses & Strains - Any workshop should start by recognising that there will be potential anatomical problems, leading to aches and pains, that can arise from the dancers' faults in physique, for example, because of small differences between the dimensions of each leg, as well as from faults in technique.

Feet - Walk around to get the feel of normal 'pronation', the natural inward rocking motion, as the foot rotates from heel to toe. One can tell if the movement is abnormal by examining the worn edges of heels or soles for evidence of any over-compensating action. There are a number of contributory sources that need individual diagnosis. 'Orthics', a form of shoe insert, are now available commercially for the correction of some faults, eg to straighten joints.

The Turn Out of the feet is a relic of the old style of movement, which remained fashionable for 300 years, till the codification of Modern Ballroom Dancing by Victor Sylvestor's committee of the 1920's. In this sense the morris can be a museum! It can have significance - McCorquadale in the Wembley Olympics in London 1948, missed a medal in the 100 yds by less than a yard, experts said because of the distance lost by the turn out of his foot whilst running. Also in this 17th century style there was the swaggering outward swing of the leg when moving either forward or back, which action incidentally allowed room for the wearing of fancy boots with lace tops etc. The movement style is still inherent in the morris backstep of several of the Cotswold village traditions.

UPS & DOWNS

Vertical Jump - You may think that it is all to do with feet and ankles but just try making one without using the major thigh muscles. The attempt demonstates the need for a bend of the knees, the 'plié', an action once considered so basic that it was simply called 'the movement'. Most of the effort and hence the velocity into a jump comes from using the big muscles in the thighs. The maximum height reached is helped by a rolling up on the toes with a full extension of the foot, as the height comes from this roll-up distance plus the velocity that has been achieved when finally leaving contact with the ground. What can be achieved is limited by the length of the foot! The further height gained in the air is limited by gravity, which pulls one down rather rapidly, so that the actual time out of contact with the ground is rather short. If the use of foot extension on the rise is limited, by shoe heel height or deliberately by the dancer, then it may not be being used by the dancer at the landing. The risk on landing is then that of jarring the leg joints, leading in the long term to the damage of cartilage and ligaments, as has happened to many of the old traditional dancers. The number of "g"s experienced in this can be as high as three. One can practice avoiding slapping the ground by trying to land quietly.

The apparent achieved height is partly an illusion. An audience sees the total body/head rise and fall, including the drop while in contact with the ground before and after the jump, which will be to below the normal standing upright starting posture position.

Stretching and Warm-Up - For both achieving the freedom of movement and the avoidance of injury, it is very desirable to start with a stretching and warm up activity, not a vigorous warm up, one should still be able to talk naturally to a neighbour whilst doing it. One should also include a warm down at the end of a dance period to avoid subsequent stiffness, dissapating the waste products in one's system. Sources for ideas are booklets such as that published by the Morris Federation and magazine articles or by talking to sports coaches for something appropriate to the actions used.

Beginners tend to tense all their muscles, so they exhaust easily. Their new movements are achieved by counterbalancing muscular forces, and this is not the same as a normal control of movement. We should work to avoid this tightness by "loosening up" the actions and relaxing the inessential muscles, but this requires confidence. Such an approach produces a visible difference in the movements, which is the 'body language' by which we can recognise "experience" in a dancer.

It is important to present visual images to learners, reinforced with words. I think that part of the general learning problem of translating words heard into movement is due to having to communicate internally between the two halves of the brain, with their different skills. The mind also forms separate "intelligences" for different activities which then have to be trained to work together. Another trick of focussing attention onto the key elements came from Douglas Kennedy who always spoke of the need to present new movements both in "close-up" and in "long-shot".

One perceives one's own movements on a different basis from how the apparently same movements look when done by others and this can be misleading. Actors on the stage exaggerate every day gestures to make them appear normal when under the undivided scrutiny of an audience at a distance. One's own gestures are often much smaller and jerky than one imagines. Actors are trained to observe accurately and to replicate what they are shown when closely observed, as on TV or films, but ordinary people unfortunately copy with a significantly smaller movement. A typical and common personal experience occurs when teaching the Longborough hand waves, actually a wrist movement, but often dancers move their hands to follow the motion appropriate to the handkerchiefs, because there is a mental image or movement analysis problem. Over a number of generations of foremen the quality of movements within a club can degrade very noticeably. It is good to work sometimes privately or in a group in front of a big mirror, ideally in a dance studio, but deep office or school windows can be adequate substitutes.

Jump - To explore the use of the arms, first swing them up together while jumping, from having the hands just behind the hips, till they are well up in front of the body and higher than the head. The opposite, of a swing down during the jump, feels quite different and less height is managed - more appropriate to a standing long jump! Incidentally this used to be a Much Wenlock Olympic, the heir to Dover's Cotswold Olympic Games at Dover's Hill, Chipping Campden, as well an early Modern Olympiad event. The world best is over 3 meters!

What is role of the arms? After all, all control is ultimately only by contact with the ground. How does this small mass effect the amount and quality of movement? It is a dynamic effect, understandable from Newton's Laws of Motion. One major interaction comes with the swing up of the arms, the total force (reaction) onto (from) the ground is increased while the arms accelerate, ie are not lifted smoothly, and the body leaves the ground with more total momentum, ie velocity.

Once off the ground the path of the body's centre of gravity is determined. All that can be varied is the relative position of the body's parts to it. Raising up the feet or bending the legs while in the air reduce the height reached by the head. Remember that half the time off the ground is spent in the upper quarter of the trajectory (near apogee, if one is a space scientist!).

For achieving the maximum height, as measured by the head's rise in the jump, one must decelerate and bring down the arms before reaching the top of the leap. The additional "apparent" height comes from the downward shift of the overall centre of gravity relative to the head.

For the appearance of a higher jump, it can be made to appear to last longer by holding the 'pose' and not bringing the arms down till touching the ground and starting into the plié, a trick that can be seen to be used in the ballet. Gravity does not allow one to actually float!

There is a team problem which arises from aiming to get people of different sizes to appear to bob up and down together. It is easy for shorter people just to rise less, whereas all should rise the same. Therefore a consensus has to be found on the height to be reached while extending the foot. Shorter footed people have to work harder! There will be subtle differences in the relative movements as the acceleration profile required depends on the foot length. A useful practice technique is to form a circle facing inwards, with each dancers arms extended sideways so that their hands are on their neighbours' shoulders. They can then be sensitive to relative height and timing differences as they dance together.

There is a nomenclature problem that can confuse beginners because "jump" is used variously in the morris to mean the take-off, the movement from take-off to landing and just the landing. Often morris dance notations will refer to a "step-&-jump" meaning a jumping off of a step and then landing. If it ends "feet-together", it means landing on both feet simultaneously with them side-by-side ("first position" to the dance teacher_.

Turns - To examine the significance of 'roll inertia', start with some non-travelling jumps, and try simple jumps begining with a 180° turn, to end facing the opposite way. Try to keep the arms down at one's sides for a few jumps, then to keep them fully extended out to the side for some more. Both are hard work, showing that arms actually do have a role. Then finally draw them in whilst turning, and after the earlier jumps, one usually find one overshoots, because the progressive drop in roll inertia keeps the angular velocity up! Normally the arms are used quite naturally, ie without conscious effort, to control the landing. Such arm control to compensate for ground friction in a turn while in continual ground contact is a part of the morris man's technique for galleys and hooks.

Keep the body straight in a jump. Of course one must thrust up through one's centre of gravity to avoid tumbling in the air, but do not stick the stomach out or arch the back. Such body movement is ugly, and, having no ground contact, is difficult to control, as well as being a significant contributor to injuries. Aerial contortions go with gymnastics, high diving and circus tumbling, but not with the morris! To turn in a jump a twist has to be given to the body by the feet and perhaps helped by an initial turn of the legs and upper body in the opposite direction to gain from unwinding as is done by ballet dancers and the Basques for complete turns in the air.

The head, although small, is also a mass that significantly affects the dynamics of one's body movements. One thing to carefully avoid is drooping it during a jump. Get someone to watch what you do. Consciously stretching the neck up would be much better.

'Spotting' is a technique for obtaining stability in a horizontal rotation. Fix the eyes on a distant point and let the head initially lag the turn, then snap the neck round, say to the final direction if doing a 180° turn. Suprisingly, by doing this one is less likely to sway in the turn. It must have something to do with the role of the inner ear in providing an attitude reference. Conventional dance pirouettes, ie turns with foot-to-ground contact, are not part of the Cotswold morris. The equivalent rotations are the galleys and hooks.

Posture is important. It is visible all the time to the audience, not just while dancing. They see the implied 'body language' and it should say "eager" and "interested" in what is going on. At rest one should be upright and balanced on the balls of the feet. Do not forget such old fashioned practice tricks as balancing a book on the head. Bringing the body weight back onto the heels for a "rest" introduces the problem of achieving snappy acceleration into the next move, as well as giving the body language message of non-participation. The overall impression looks slack and suggests sloppy morris. When all of a side does it, it tells the audience that it is an interval during which their attention can wander. Dancers can be trained in posture and other body language messages.

A rigid torso seems characteristic of Cotswold morris. There are traditionally few flexible movements of the body other than a twist about the vertical with some of the 'side steps'.

There is the issue of the optimum height for heels on shoes, as yet unresolved. The best position for the foot is with the heel just off the ground and this is reflected in shoe design. A heel offers a better posture in a relaxed position. But shoe heels reduce the available flexure at the ankle joint. In England there is commonly a difference in the choice of shoes between the sexes. Most European folk dancers favour a very light weight dance shoe, equivalent to that used by the Scots, with little or no heel - but one must remember that the Bluebell Girls, Can-Can dancers and persons like Ginger Rogers could manage quite a lot on high heels!

A well designed shoe would have shock absorbing material under the ball of the foot, but those worn never do. It is common to have a stiff sole to cope with the wide variety of dance surfaces. "Trainers" seem to lead to the appearance of dancing "pigeon-toed" due to both the different cut of the shoe and the way support is provided.

Breath - This should be 'abdominal' with an outward stomach movement, not pulled in as one breathes in, as this leads to 'stitch', because then the diaphragm is working the wrong way. The pain is actually the muscle spasms. To avoid it, it helps to take some deep breaths before starting, these also assist both poise and readiness. Actors use this technique to control their nerves before stage entries. Once a woman at a workshop concentrated so hard that she did not breathe at all during a dance, she went blue and had to be taken to a hospital for oxygen to ensure recovery!

Let us go back to the jump to bring more of the elements together and try it with the "up-&-out" Longborough type arm movements. Start with the elbows bent at right angles and the upper arm horizontal with the hands out by the sides of the head above ear level. Raise the hands up, straightening the arms and opening them out during the jump, to end, on the landing, with both the arms horizontal and out to the side of the body palms upwards.

Where does the beat of the music come in a jump? Certainly to just touch down on landing on beat - but when on the take off? Surely not as one loses contact with the ground? The note of the music is of necessity of finite length as it has to be heard, the "beat" is the maximum stress perceived at its leading edge. The maximum effort is on the beat, but the full movement is across the beat, hence its physical and psychological appeal as a form of self expression. To get the effort timed accurately there must be anticipatory preparatory effort. Jumps need preparation, they need time to accelerate the body, and, as a jump is usually longer in the air than a step, the musician often stretches the music (and most significantly never catches up again!).

Jumps (and turns) on the move require consideration of additional technical points about the appropriate body tilts. These are dynamic situations requiring a more subtle understanding of motion. A forward drive into a travelling movement comes from being off balance, thus one should land from a jump leaning into the direction in which one wants to move off.

The initial emphasis so far has been on jumping because it leads to a desired style for the "morris stepping".

TRAVELLING

The movement possibilities are determined by the floor surface and the Cotswold Morris follows the style of stepping that was first developed at the Rennaisance. James Burke's TV series and his book "Connections" discussed the change in building style following a worsening of the average weather in the early Middle Ages and the consequential appearance of flatter floors as social life moved indoors. Before the change, the most available flat surfaces were the barn threshing floors, realistic for social but not for ritual or ceremonial dancing. Incidentally social dancing was often used to consolidate new surfaces.

Unfortunately "Step" is used colloquially in the folk dance world both for a single movement and for a sequence.

Step - Classically the basic movement is a quick change from the weight on one foot to onto the other. The style was described in the earliest dancing books and was not a knee lifting as was the medieval outdoor 'clod-hopping'. The knee lift that is typical of the traditional Engligh country dancing and other seasonal dance traditions presumably developed to avoid physical contact with partners and neighbours on small crowded dance floors. Start by standing on the ball of one foot with the other in the air, about the length of the foot in front of the supporting foot. The free foot is kept about horizontal and relaxed during the movement and with the toes neither curled up ('Turkish Harem') or pointed down ('Schoolgirl Ballet'). Really it is irrelevant to practice stepping on one spot as one is seldom dancing without travelling, and then only with some special emphasis required. A little thought will show that real movement sequences involving stepping usually start from jumps or otherwise having the feet together, but this introduces a complication at a first teaching of the steps which is well avoided. Although it is natural to start practicing with very little lift, the early development of a reasonable amount of spring in the step is essential.   Remember the insult meant by the phrase "weak-kneed"!

In the Cotswold Morris it is customary to have the musician play a 4 or 8 bar phrase as a 'Once-to-Yourself' before starting to dance. It focuses the dancers attention, captures the audience and allows the team to check and absorb the speed and rhythm.

6/8 Jig Time - Try two "steps" per bar (almost capers, which are the same action as a 'step' but with a greater lift and usually a more exaggerated arm movement) - also start from standing on one foot. To help keep them "symmetrical", ie with equal effort off each foot, start by accompanying them using circular waves of both arms, at one per step, with the stress or emphasis on the upward rise or "lift". "Up" in a step or a spring takes longer than "Down" due to the directionality of the effect of gravity.   The tune's rhythm is important. Compare a jig in 6/8 with a hornpipe in 4/4. There is less life in dancing the latter as the more even rhythm constrains the body rise that is possible. True polkas, as distinct from polka tunes played as hornpipes, have an irregular rhythm (they fit the clog morris polka well) and are best avoided with beginners, because they induce bad dance habits. Marches in 2/4 or 6/8 have a different feel yet again.

What is a good morris tune? It needs to be able to be played to fit the effort profile of the movement sequence, in particularly to stress the lift on the first beats.   Modern tunes do not lend themselves to matching this movement characteristic.

Traditions surviving into the 20th century have acquired an off-beat emphasis, with a strong movement on the weak beats (this was first a rhythm called a Schottische). Although no Ragtime or subsequent popular musical style has stuck with the morris (ignoring some individual and limited examples, eg Eclectic Morris). It has led to the villages teaching a basic single step with a foot lift up and a kick forward style, which is not the classical stepping style recognised by Sharp that has been introduced here.

The jig rhythm encourages hops. Starting from the simple capers, put in the hops, still keeping the action symmetrical with each free foot travelling forward the same distance and the body rise being the same off of either foot. The drive is off the ball of the foot, just like the jumps.

Look out of a window and watch the relative motion of the horizontal frame or bars against the outdoor scene as an indication of ones own body motion. There are 4 rises per bar, the first and third are larger than the second and fourth. These main beats are called the "Strong" and those in between the "Weak" beats.

To get a feel of the meaning of differences between "traditions" and of the problems facing beginners, try repeating this simple stepping with appropriately different arm movements.

1.   Down & Up both arms in parallel, (Hinton) in vertical plane

2.   Alternate Arms as in exaggerated walking (Chipping Campden)

3.   Forward Flick of both hands together (Bampton)

4.   Low Circular Waves forward facing, at side, (Brackley) in vertical plane at hip level

5.   High Circular Waves at mid chest level (Badby) in vertical plane

Note the feeling of a "help" on the UP part of the arm movement. A natural consequence is that vigorous arm down swings do not contribute to height but a feeling of lightness and that a gentle drop is preferred to snatches when seeking lift. Thus the character of the movement as perceived by the new dancer will depend on the tradition being taught.

Any Arming Sequence - Do it first without the associated stepping but simulating the body bounce. Beginners can have a problem of coordinating arm, leg and body movements new to them so there is some value in a little practice of these separately. Because of the additional problem of stepping and arming coordination, practice arm sequences alone for a while to obtain the flow, but not for too long, as they are slightly modified by the body actions when actually stepping. Note that there is an artistic opinion that good dancers would not move their hands in front of the their face to cover an important informative part of the image being presented to the audience.

A Left Foot Lead is of medieval origin. Then they danced in a linked curved line and moved first to the left and then to the right. The left foot lead, as with the military march, is natural because it is actually a thrust off of the nominally stronger right foot to get moving off smartly. To go with the sun was lucky, to start to windershins, as supposedly did witches, was not.

Left handed people are at a little disadvantage in the morris. Some such dancers can be slower at picking up directional calls. The major problem appears to be with using the right hand for holding and manipulating sticks.

Form a set of 6 dancers, in two files of 3, numbered 1, 3, 5 (the "odds") in the left hand column, and 2, 4, 6 (the "evens") in the right, and all facing "up" towards the music. The numbering is as for the then familiar teams of horses, with No 1 being "foremost" and No 6 "hindmost".

Perhaps a word is needed about the morris compass. "Up" is towards the musician who conventionally stands at the "top" end of the set by dancers numbers 1 and 2. "Down" is the other way, towards the "bottom" of the set. Confusingly "Up and Down" are also used for arm movements. Facing one's opposite is "in" or "across the set", and turns towards that direction are "inward". The contrary is "out" and turning that way "outward".

Try dancing a very simple but illustrative set dance, derived from Chipping Campden's "Constant Billy". The following is a condensed dance description. For a better understanding of the terminology, try consulting the Morris Federation's published "Glossary of Terms".

Face one's opposite across the set for the playing of a 'Once To Yourself', then jump and turn 90° in the air to face left, odds facing up, and evens facing down in the last bar. The whole set dance a complete 'whole rounds' clockwise in 8 bars, ending as at the once to yourself by facing across the set, and continuing by approaching one's opposite in 4 bars to be within an arm's reach, ending the move with a jump to stand with one's feet together side by side, and facing one's opposite. Clap hands with the opposite dance as described below, then dance past one's opposite, passing by the left shoulder. Turn to the right in a small loop by oneself in the opposite's starting place to face back and approach again etc. Repeat the crossing and clapping a few times, then end the dance with the opening 'whole rounds' figure again.

The Clapping is, bar 1 both own hands together in front of one's chest, partners clap r+r,

bar 2 both own hands together again, partners clap l+l,

bar 3 both own hands, clap both own hands together behind one's back,

bar 4 both own hands together, finally r+l & l+r simultaneously

  : in the obvious but brief notation used by Sharp and Bacon.

6/8 Double Step - This is 3 quick changes and a hop, "1 2 3 hop", with the "lift" on the hop. The broken rhythm ensures an unequal rise on the 4 movements. Lack of thought can lead to an uneven forward kick - it needs to be an equal distance with either foot. The "correct" distance forward was once a bone of contention in the national press between rival collectors!

There are 'Double' and 'Single' steps, the terminology comes from Tudor times when they were called a double and a single (or simple). For the Single step the lead (first strong beat of each bar) is always off the same foot through a musical phrase. For the Double there is a changing, ie alternating, lead.

The double step in 4/4 feels different to that in 6/8. There are several rhythms conventionally given a 4/4 (or 2/4) signature besides the reels, called variously hornpipes, schottisches, polkas, rants, measures or marches. Each produces a different feel to the dance movements, once the dancer is sensitive to them, because of the differing time constraints on the "lift" that is possible in the stepping. The simple rhythm implied is not precise because Morris musicians typically stretch the melody's rhythm to better fit the morris movements. The previous exercise with various arm movements should be repeated. The alternate arm swinging is difficult to fit to double steps!

The short time out of contact from the ground reflects the power of gravity, therefore one should fully exploit using the foot extension and the initial and final bend at the knee to control height and speed. The question of speed of the dance coupled with achievable stepping height is a matter of the physical effort level that can be maintained.

One of our difficulties today is that we assume that the morris is usually danced with a classic form of the double or single steps and for many traditions this has to do by default of better knowledge. Unfortunately where we know something of the manner of performance and of its local teaching there does appears significant variation.

For single stepping ("hops") :

Bampton :   lift the free foot straight upwards, then kick it forward and somewhat down off the top of the lift, and the bells ring twice on the off beat at the acceleration and deceleration of the lower leg - this can be called "pedalling".

Campden :   ditto but with a longer forward thrust of the free leg and aiming at only one ring of the bells, giving a very irregular or "broken" rhythm.

Bidford :   the first move is a low kick forward, then a lift as the foot is brought back - this can be called "back-pedalling".

Headington : the leg is kept fairly straight throughout, the movement made quickly and the posture held for the hop.

The contrast with other seasonal custom styles can be emphasised, eg the Flamborough Long Sword and some Border styles with their high knee lift and no kick forward, and the common current Border interpretation of drawing the free foot back so that the kick forward hardly passes the supporting leg.

There is a problem in persuading most people of the degree of effort that is involved in performing the morris.

Fitness - This consists of three elements, stamina, flexibility and strength. Most of us are not physically fit! Something more than a once a week session is considered by experts to be necessary to achieve and maintain a modest level of general fitness (three 20 minutes sessions is often recommended). How many people have the time or the inclination to exercise vigorously three times a week? Only the committed few. But you can not store up fitness, if you stop exercising the benefits gradually disappear. The typical once weekly morris practice therefore is inadequate on its own. Other sessions of perhaps different physical activity (not particularly exercise) should be added, such as brisk walks, swimming, cycling etc. It is important that you feel good afterwards so that it is kept up. You may of course have specific needs which may have to be met by an organised training schedule. Given our national lethargy, few people are at risk of doing too much!

There should be a general concern for the state of the muscles that resist gravity. The back and leg muscles develop with dancing, therefore the opposite muscles need strengthening - the abdominal (eases back pain), the shin area (eases shin splints) and the thigh area (eases knee pain).

'Shin Splints' is a common complaint and it arises from abnormal strain and stress on the muscles and tendons that lift the forefoot, control the toes, and absorb shock and stabilise the foot during foot plant on the floor. Often the condition comes from being unused to being on the balls of the feet, or from over-striding, from tension during the foot swing, leaning forward or not having well cushioned shoes, ie dancing on too hard a floor for the footwear. Even experienced dancers have this condition when they dramatically increase their activity or develop muscle imbalance.

There are several alleviating actions that might be taken. Wearing thicker soled shoes, not slapping the floor with the foot sole, having a more upright posture, and relaxing the free foot when it is out of contact with the ground are possibilities. Alternatively, or additionally, so are using stretching exercises for the calf, hamstring and Achilles tendon, exercising by lifting objects with the toes, and checking that clothing is not too tight around the legs eg from elastic bands or bell pads (or practicing in unsuitable jeans).

The pain could be an indication of a more major condition so it must be taken seriously. The major clue is the time it takes to subside. The worst but rather rare condition needs an operation within hours for complete recovery.

Actions on Injury - The best advice is, if it hurts, it is telling you something! Be aware of the serious risk of "dancing through" a pain.

Strains and sprains are best dealt with immediately by ice packs (even the commercial equivalent of frozen pea packets), and blisters by puncture and plasters, but not by removal of the skin.

At a guess, of all the sports, Cotswold Morris has an affinity with Basketball, because of the turns during the running and jumping, and hence there is a similarity of rotational stress on joints and muscles which is not so common in other sports.   More examination of relevant experience in other sports could be done to the advantage of understanding the physical problems associated with the morris eg footwear, types of injury, and fitness training. Athletic shoes are often designed with jogging movements in mind, with cushioning of the heel which takes the impact in gentle running, rather than any cushioning of the ball of the foot that takes the battering in the morris.

A Sequence of Steps should be seen and practiced as the basic unit of movement.   It involves integrating the jump and usually significantly different forward and back steps.

Try the following simple "Princess Royal", a very basic version of the jig but from no village in particular. It is best learnt by following someone demonstrating it.

The order is Foot-Up, Jig, Plain Capers, Jig, Slow Capers, and a final Jig, using the conventional terms for the steps and sections of the dance. Some movements are discussed in more detail later.

Foot-Up   =   6 double steps, 2 single steps used as backsteps and a jump, landing feet together.

Jig- long open sidestep to the left (2 bars) and to the right   or chorus (2 bars), 2 double steps on the spot, "cross stepping" for 2 bars, left foot crossed over right, both apart and crossed again, then pause for a beat. In reverse, right foot crossed over left, apart and cross again and pause. 2 double steps on the spot, 2 single steps as backsteps and a jump (12 bars in all).

Plain Capers- 8 Plain Capers on the spot, 2 double steps, 2 single steps as backsteps and a jump.

Slow Capers- 4 slows to the same tune but played somewhat slower for the first 4 bars. Cross the feet, first the left in front, then the right in front, bring the feet together and jump forward, landing with both feet together. This is done 4 times etc, with arm movements corresponding to the feet : "out to side", "out", "up-and-over" to "out" again.

As a guide the angle between the feet, when the heels are close together and the toes apart, has to be sufficient to allow a twisting of the individual feet on their balls, so that the heel of the foot being twisted inward can clear the other supporting foot. In the classical ballet the customary turn out is very large and it needs a training from an early age to achieve the joint mobility. In Old Tyme dancing it is 90° (originally perhaps to avoid treading on the hems of long dresses), and this was normal in social dancing till an English Modern Ballroom dance committee, led by Victor Silvester in the early 1920's, decided on a parallel stance. In the morris the turn out matters in some sidesteps and backsteps but not necessarily during the basic "stepping". The turn-out looks "tidy" when one is standing still and is a stable starting point for movement off in any direction.

Backstep - A similar body movement to that in the ordinary stepping but with different emphases. The body rise is much less and there is a stronger sink down. At most traditional places except Badby the backstep were singles. Often the free foot is not lifted off the ground but slid or scuffed backwards. This downward emphasis applies even to the accompanying waves of the arms. One should now attempt the Fieldtown basic stepping and arming sequence with the small figure of eight path wave and rotation of the hands during the backsteps going "out&down - in&over - out&down".

Capers - The next energetic step to be met is the "caper" from one foot to the other. The Cotswold tradition is distinguished from the others as having dances with "jumps and capers". From one point of view a simple caper can be thought of as arising out of the basic 'double-step' when one individual step is so strong that it is not followed by a step or hop on the next weak beat. A series of these energetic changes are called plain capers. If after landing on the other foot, the caper is followed by a hop on that same foot, then the sequence is called a Half Caper, or sometimes a Spring Caper, and during a sequence of them the lead is always off with the same foot. If it is followed by a change of step it is called a Furrie or Furry and during a sequence of them the lead off is off of alternate feet. Capers off and onto the same foot are seldom met in the Cotswold Morris (perhaps they occurred in Oddington slows).

The choice of the accompanying arm movements to be used with the plain or half capers, eg "up-and-down" or "down-and-up", affects the stress, feel, and appearance of the movement.

Double Step Sequences - In a finer analysis each individual step has a different emphasis. For example to put in the travel, one must accelerate, move, decelerate, stop, reverse, etc. finally stopping again. Watch another dancer move. The body rotates and leans forward and backwards as a function of the acceleration and deceleration, particularly during the backstep and jump. Using gravity again to move one's centre of gravity forward, the body slopes to move, then one moves the feet to stop falling over, the same principle as satellites use in the earth's gravity field. Some authorities say that one should lean forward during a backstep which is never a rushing movement and does not need the same degree of drive, but does need the preparation for the final jump.

One needs to note again the rotation of the body in the air to prepare for moving off from a jump, often a difficult point. Be aware of landing a foot's length behind the stationary position. This allows a snappy move off. Practice by standing with the heels against a line on the floor and on the jump land with the toes against that same line (the feet being entirely on the other side).

THE REST

Let us end the exercises described by trying a Longborough style sidestep dance. The dance is constructed of 4 figures, each followed by the same chorus. For this workshop, the figures are danced with a 4 bar stepping sequence which is essentially the same, other than being a mirror image, for both halves of the figures. The sequence is a double step and a jump moving forwards, then backsteps (or single steps), and another jump moving back. The sequence starts with stepping onto the "outside foot", usually the left first, and the right in the second halves.

The figures are,

Foot up - all face "up". After the Once to Yourself, dance the defined sequence, turning "outwards", away from one's opposite, to face "down" on the second jump. Repeat the sequence facing down, but turning "inwards", the 'easy way', on the second jump, to face one's opposite.

Half Gip - all face across set. Dance past each other, passing right shoulders and then retire backwards to place along the same path, then repeat to the other side of one's opposite passing left shoulders.

Back-to-Back - as the half-gip, but having passed one's opposite, move behind them to be able to retire backwards passing the other shoulder. Repeat going past this other shoulder first.

Whole Gip - as the back-to-back, but done as a face-to-face, so that on the first jump, turn to face back across the set, then single step forwards, passing by the same shoulder, to the jump to face across again still turning the same way. Repeat in the reverse direction.

Each chorus is a sidestep sequence followed by a half hey that inverts the order of the dancers in the set, without changing sides, which sequence is then repeated to bring all the dancers back to where they started the chorus.

Sidestep - It is probable that each village had its own interpretation of this particular "step" sequence. The feet could be crossed or apart, the body turned a little or a lot, with one arm or both in use, and the handkerchief action could be at different levels and of the various types often based on wrist actions. The sidestep can be long (2 bars) or a mixture of sidesteps, double steps and jumps (or even a hook into a hey).

A sidestep is strictly a movement only half a bar long whether "crossed" or "open". A "short" sidestep is a bar long and is either a sidestep followed by a step and a hop with the feet side by side like a double step, or it is one repeated if to be followed by a full double step. A "long" sidestep takes two bars and is in effect the second short form followed by the first form.

As for most traditions at Longborough the relative angle between the feet, the "turn out", is maintained throughout the sidestep, and the forward foot is not turned to be more parallel with the other. The feet are crossed over with the heel of the leading foot in the air but close to the toe of the rear one, and the body is turned no more than 30-45° following the direction of the crossing of the feet. The forward or "leading" arm only is raised, and this is usually carried fairly straight up past the ear. Like in all Cotswold traditions, the sidestep should be performed very energetically. For this practice, cross the feet for one bar, dance a double step straight, cross the feet the other way, and dance another straight double.

The traditional Cotswold morris does not have movements that "drive" the body into the floor. However many sides teach sidesteps with a pronounced dip in the arm wave and with the body. People have to make up their own mind as to what is acceptable within their own team's performance but the dip is ugly, lazy and untraditional.

In the Half Hey the opposite dancers work in pairs. The path pattern is described here in sequence but is performed simultaneously. The top pair turn out and dance down the side of the set to the bottom place. They must turn and come down the set quickly such that the jump in the second bar can be made travelling sideways. The stepping in the third bar is a galley, not backsteps, with the dancers rotating away from the centre line of the set and moving out to the final position. At the same time the middle pair follow the top pair round, in the first half hey moving to the top of the set, but turning out quickly so that the jump can be back to where they started, going no more up than the top pair's starting place. The middles should leave just enough space between themselves and the tops to let the bottoms pass through. The bottoms move to face down and turn out to come up to the top, going behind the tops, but passing in front of the middles.

Diagonals lines appearing in body actions are more interesting to watch than verticals. The recent drift to vertical arm/hand movements in developing new traditions can only be justified in terms of appearing different rather than in being artistically better. Be conscious of leading the sidestep hand movements with the wrist, also of controling the direction of the eyes which often affects one's posture, particularly of the head. The smile is an important visual with many gradations of interpretation by the audience, so it must appear genuine and not forced.

Work now on examples of the various side step arm gestures from Cotswold traditions. The similarities and differences must be pointed out. Here is list.

One   handed Waist high low circular wave at side Adderbury, Ilmington

One handed	Chest high circular wave at side	Brackley, Badby
Two handed	Chest high circular waves	Abingdon
One handed	Vertical countertwist circles	Bledington
One handed	Waves forward towards opposite	Bidford
One handed	High twists	Ascott, Sherborne
Two handed	High twists	Headington Quarry
Two handed	Twists at different levels	Wheatley
One handed	Full arm swing across body	Ducklington
One handed (Woodley)	Full arm swing forward and down	Bampton
Two handed (Shergold)	Waist high wave & push forward	Bampton
One handed	Swing up from side to face	Oddington
One handed	Point, up in straight line	Bucknell, Fieldtown
Two handed	Both up on middle beat	Kirtlington

Mechanics of Movement - These are often not at all simple, for example consider what happens in high diving competition, in circus tumbling and in the landing of a falling cat. We have met the effect of arm inertia in jumps and of roll inertia in a jump and turn. Drive in the galley or hook comes from reducing the roll inertia during the rotation. By starting with the arms extended, the body tilted into the turn, and the upper part of the free leg raised, the roll inertia can be 4 times that when the body is vertical and with the arms at the sides. As the dancer turns the arms are brought in, the body made more vertical and the free leg lowered. The lower part of the free leg is twisted once or twice in the turn and this motion can be used to help the dancer to turn. School learnt applied mathematics is of some use after all! Of course different villages had different detail in their ways of performing this movement. At Longborough they kept the thigh up and horizontal, turning smoothly and making the first step bisect the total angle of turn. At Bledington they went for a low sweep and at Sherborne they made the first step without a turn at all.

Team Issues - There are issues that arise from being in a team. Morris is one of the few activities that require all the participants to work together for the result, like change ringing on church bells, and each has to compromise with their ability to achieve the "togetherness". For an example of another issue there is the rhythm, speed and togetherness of stick tapping. Sticking choruses seem to have the problem of achieving acceleration into the next movement, dancers often forget to be up on their toes and to make a preparatory lift into the move off.

Technique with Sticks - No matter how good the technique one must start with a good stick. Willow makes the best sticks as it gives a good sound, is resilient and splinters safely. It should be cut over long, after the sap has stopped rising, and stored for six months or more horizontally on the flat to prevent bowing. Green wood is untrustworthy. It should be cut to the required length when needed. In the 19th century morris one usually provided one's own stick, on pain of a fine. They were often painted and shorter than normal today.

The grip is mostly with the thumb and forefinger, the rest of the hand provides the control and rotation. The fingers should tighten their grip at the moment of impact with another stick. This allows a good sound, bounce and control, and is safer because of the lack of a follow through movement. Hits should normally be upward, not across or downward. Clashes can be preceded by a large arm movement and rotation of the stick for effect but exaggerated movement does not mean great force.

Adderbury sticks are somewhat longer than other village's and are held and used differently. In "singles" the stick is held in the middle by the right hand and the stick is moved by a combination of rotation of the lower arm from the elbow and the fingers and the wrist. In "doubles", held in both hands, the butt pivots in the left hand which only moves a little, while the right hand does the stick rotation. The right hand slides along the stick as is necessary for each movement.

The worst performed and ugliest movement in the morris is the turn to face away from one's opposite and raising one's stick in both hands overhead to receive a stick hit. Thought must be given to the associated foot movements for balance and appearance. The body posture should be upright and not bent over backwards. The stick should be held up in the air above the head and not behind it. This ensures that the hitting stick is not aimed at the head. A similar principle works for offering a stick up horizontally in front of the body. It should be high enough that the stick appears to cover the eyes of one's opposite when looking across the set. It is not part of the morris to hide the stick tapping from the audience, so all tapping should be reasonably high, and impacts points should be at eye level or above.

Dancers should listen to the music and follow the phrasing in tapping. They can avoid speeding up by making larger movements between taps. Pushing the music shows inexperience and possibly a lack of constructive practice.

The sticks are carried in different ways for each tradition, vertically in front, vertically at the side with the arm down at the side with the tip either up or down, or horizontally, the choice usually depending on the stick length. Whether the stick is swung with the normal or a reduced arm movement in stepping and jumps is also dependent on the tradition. The choice should be dominated first by safety and then by appearance considerations.

Ons-&-Offs - Many sides let themselves down with their exits and entries, and even as they prepare for 'Once-to-Yourself' before the dance starts and also in the manner in which they behave immediately after 'all-in' or 'all-up' at the end of a dance.

Dance is Style - Remember the importance of body language and be aware of being on "stage" and visible all of the time.

The details of style are "personal" as well as "club" and will need a direct one-to-one working out between the beginner and their teacher. Dancers have to learn to spread the physical effort over all the muscles, using the shoulders and back as well as the arms and legs. There is a similarity with the actions of professional craftsman, eg like a carpenter working with a plane who does not work just with his arms.

There is an old story that the audience can only recognise a few dances, the tunes and movements seeming so similar. It is so often true because no contrast is being provided between dances or even using the opportunities within a dance. Dances can be presented as ceremonial, athletic or funny. Showmanship suggests that contrasts within and between dances are exploited. The dances and the show can have a structure and a climax.

There is no substitute for directly observing other morris dancers and sides critically both for the lessons from their good and their bad points. Much can be learnt from recognising what is wrong about other performances!

Men and/or Women - There are obvious physical differences, in average height and weight (fat) distribution and in physical strength, but the major effect in mixed sets is the women's smaller feet, for the same overall height, making matching of the shape of the vertical movement difficult. There are also differences in postures and positioning between the sexes ('body language' again). There can be differences in fitness and muscle control which can be avoided by training. Women can have a lower self-esteem, which shows up in behaviour during public performance and in weak stick handling. Awareness of the problems can lead to action to overcome all such consequences which are mostly cultural not physical.

Long and Short People - Traditionally teams were lucky is they had 6 good dancers, they were often pleased to have 3 to put on one side. Such teams perhaps encouraged a spread in individual performance which covered the lack of uniformity. Disparity is a problem. As dancers work primarily in pairs, matching within the pairs is an obvious possibility. The proper dimensions of a set reflect the average dancer's size with typical fingertip-to-fingertip separation in both directions. Consequently, short people have to scamper around and long people amble.

Note : words enclosed in '-' are specialist usages, those in "-" are slang or jargon.

RETROSPECT
Poor morris through ignorance is inexcusable. But there are many acceptable forms that deviate from the classical styles. There are several reasons why this may be desirable or necessary. If each is thought through then it is difficult to be critical. What has to be avoided is such poor morris that it gives the rest of morris a bad name. Unfortunately those who do it never seem to understand what is objectional in what they do.

MORRIS MANNERS
Once outside dancing to an audience it is desirable to observe the good manners of the morris. Do not stand in front of the audience

when not dancing - the show is for them not you. Do recognise that people who read posters may not understand morris time. ©1992 R L Dommett

V 3.4Cotswold Basics ©1992 R L Dommett